Table of Contents

Top 20 Test Taking Tips

1. Carefully follow all the test registration procedures
2. Know the test directions, duration, topics, question types, how many questions
3. Setup a flexible study schedule at least 3-4 weeks before test day
4. Study during the time of day you are most alert, relaxed, and stress free
5. Maximize your learning style; visual learner use visual study aids, auditory learner use auditory study aids
6. Focus on your weakest knowledge base
7. Find a study partner to review with and help clarify questions
8. Practice, practice, practice
9. Get a good night's sleep; don't try to cram the night before the test
10. Eat a well balanced meal
11. Know the exact physical location of the testing site; drive the route to the site prior to test day
12. Bring a set of ear plugs; the testing center could be noisy
13. Wear comfortable, loose fitting, layered clothing to the testing center; prepare for it to be either cold or hot during the test
14. Bring at least 2 current forms of ID to the testing center
15. Arrive to the test early; be prepared to wait and be patient
16. Eliminate the obviously wrong answer choices, then guess the first remaining choice
17. Pace yourself; don't rush, but keep working and move on if you get stuck
18. Maintain a positive attitude even if the test is going poorly
19. Keep your first answer unless you are positive it is wrong
20. Check your work, don't make a careless mistake

Theatre

Elements of acting

Relaxation, concentration, imagination, and observation:
There are several schools of thought about the qualities that one must either naturally possess or work to acquire in order to be an actor. The elements of relaxation, concentration, imagination and observation are most common among these qualities. An actor must maintain control of voice and body while performing and this ability is compromised by nervousness. Actors must learn to force their minds and bodies into a state of relaxation. Concentration allows the actor to focus attention on the desired outcome. Actors must use their voices and bodies in a way that conveys the essence of the character. An actor who is properly concentrating on the role will think about what they are doing rather than how they are doing it. Actors must also be mindful of the full range of human emotion. They must observe the manifestations of emotions in themselves and others and use these memories while performing. The actor should also be able to imagine the joys and sufferings of their characters, conveying that through performance.

Preparing for performance

Psychologically and emotionally:
The concept of the "magic if" is often an effective tool used by actors. The *magic if* theory requires that actors imagine they are in the character's situation. These scenarios can be played out in two ways. Actors can be themselves but act as if they were in the same situation as characters or they can act as if they are the characters. In the first method, actors react to the situation personally. Once they have mastered their own personal reactions, actors can then analyze their reactions and examine how these compare to what the character would do in that situation. By combining the two reactions actors can often give the most believable performance. It is also helpful to draw upon sense memory and emotional memory to be able to depict a realistic emotion or reaction during a performance.

Alexander Technique

The Alexander Technique was developed by Shakespearean orator and actor Frederick Matthias Alexander. The technique arose from Alexander's desire to overcome his chronic laryngitis. Alexander discovered that he held unnecessary muscular tension while performing which caused his vocal problems. His technique requires that actors become aware of the tension they hold in their necks while performing. By releasing the neck tension, the head relaxes and allows the spine to remain long and uncompressed. This simple physical alignment results in an overall healthy condition of the body. The technique attempts to rid the body of tension and stress through the alteration of one's daily physical movements. Tension blocks an actor's ability to effectively portray the characters and stories in a performance. Studying the Alexander Technique can help an actor to reduce the amount of tension in their bodies and better understand how energy should be allocated to certain tasks in order to most efficiently accomplish one's goals in both acting and daily life.

James-Lange theory of emotion

The James-Lange theory was developed by psychologist William James and physiologist Carl Lange. The theory states that emotions are a result of physiological response to external stimuli. Our emotions, according to this theory, are based on our interpretations of physical sensation. For example, if we are at the beach and see a shark while swimming, our body becomes tense and our heart races. We interpret these physical reactions as fear. The theory suggests that emotion is not the cause of a physical response, but the result. This can be incorporated into acting techniques by having students describe or act out physical symptoms while other students guess the corresponding emotion. Nervous actors may also be taught to physically force themselves to relax, which, according to this theory, would result in a more calm emotional state. The theory can also be used to predict emotional reactions after observing one's physical behavior.
20090427.41480.844

Cannon-Bard theory of emotion

The Cannon-Bard theory was developed by psychologists Walter Cannon and Philip Bard. Their theory states that emotion results in a physiological response, suggesting that our emotional reaction to external stimuli in turn leads to a physiological reaction. For example, feeling fearful may cause our heart to race and our body to tremble. This theory is in direct opposition of the James-Lange theory, which suggests that emotion is the result of physiological reaction and not the cause. The Cannon-Bard theory states that one must feel an emotion before the body can physiologically react. This theory can be incorporated into acting techniques by having students participate in scenarios that may make them fearful, anxious, angry or excited and then having

them describe the physiological symptoms which accompanied each emotion.

Delsarte system of expression

Francois Delsarte is best known for his system of expression involving the holding of specific poses to convey emotion or attitudes. The method was used in the first acting school founded in the United States. Delsarte began his career as a disgruntled student at the Paris Conservatory. Unsatisfied with the conservatory's acting classes, Delsarte began to independently study human movement and behavior. He also studied anatomical medicine, voice, breath and body language. All of his observations were conducted with the aim of understanding the role played by these various components as tools of instinctual and emotional expression. Delsarte's work was introduced to the US by his protégé, Steele Mackaye. Delsarte's system consists of nine principles of gesture, the relationship of inner experience and physical manifestation and the symbolism of various lines and their connection to human awareness.

Meisner technique

The goal of the *Meisner technique* has often been described as getting actors to "live truthfully under imaginary circumstances." The technique emphasizes carrying out an action truthfully on stage and letting emotion and subtext build based on the truth of the action and on the other characters around them, rather than simply playing an action or emotion. One of the most well known exercises of the Meisner Technique is called *Repetition*. In Repetition, one person spontaneously makes a comment based on their partner's behavior, and that phrase would be repeated back and forth between the two in the same manner until it changed on its own. The objective is always to react truthfully and not merely change because it felt like change was called for.

Role-playing

In role-playing, participants adopt and act out the roles of characters, or parts, that may have personalities, motivations, and backgrounds different from their own. Role-playing is like being in an improvisational drama or free-form theater in which the participants are the actors and the audience. People use the phrase "role-playing" in at least three distinct ways:

- To refer to the playing of roles generally such as in a theater, or educational setting.
- To refer to a wide range of games including computer role-playing games, play-by-mail games and more.
- To refer specifically to role-playing games.

Children's games

Children's games that involve role-play generally require no specific props and have no rules other than to stay in character. They are normally fun and can sometimes also serve the purpose of allowing children to explore adult roles and relationships. Play can reveal a lot about a child's psychological state, perception of gender roles, home life and interpretation of the world around them. Examples of common games include:

Historical re-enactment

Role-playing in the form of historical re-enactment has been practiced by adults for millennia as well. The ancient Romans, the Han Chinese and medieval Europeans all enjoyed occasionally organizing events in which everyone pretended to be from an earlier age, and entertainment appears to have been the primary purpose of these activities. Within the 20th century,

Cowboys & Indians: This game remains popular around the world, even though the films, television series, and books that might have been thought to give rise to it have largely fallen from prominence. This gives an insight into the child's perception of good and evil.
Cops & Robbers: Similar to Cowboys & Indians, seen by some as the politically correct version.
House: The main aim is to explore familial relationships. Children can act like a family and explore other family arrangements with each other. It also deals with gender roles.
Shopkeeper and Customer: This is interpretation of basic social interaction and can also be an insight into the child's parent's income status.

Improvisational theatre tradition

Another role-playing tradition is the *improvisational theatre tradition*. This goes back in some sense to the Commedia dell'Arte tradition of 16th century. Modern improvisational theatre began in the classroom with the "theatre games" of Viola Spolin and Keith Johnstone in the 1950s. Viola Spolin, who was one of the founders the famous comedy troupe Second City, insisted that her exercises were games, and that they involved role-playing, as early as 1946. She thought of these exercises as training actors and comics rather than as being primarily aimed at being fun in their own right.

historical reenactment was often pursued as a hobby.

Character analysis

In order to play the part of any character, an actor should undergo a character analysis, which is the process by which the actor learns about the unique elements that make up the character. A character can consist of vocal patterns, physical appearances, mannerisms, feelings, prejudices, aspirations, emotions and goals. The actor must study or think about all of these elements and the degree to which each of these elements are integrated within the character. The actor should try to understand the character's relationship with others, their psychological thought process, their weaknesses and strengths, their sense of morality and their history. The actor must also consider the character's place in the story and how or if the character will be changed by the events of the story.

Character development

Externals refer to the elements that an actor can use in their environment to aid in creating specific characters. An external can be a costume, a vocal change, makeup or a set of mannerisms. For many actors, externals are the primary tools used to create a character. By dressing or speaking the way a character would, the actor can begin to relate to the feelings that the character would experience. Using externals to create a character is a method called "outside-in." This means that the actor uses *outside* elements to cause *internal* changes. In order to be a character actor, one must be able to shed the restrictions of an everyday persona. They must be able to essentially create a blank slate upon which the new character can be created.

Alienation effect

The *alienation effect* is a device that is used to remind the audience that they are watching a play. While many dramatists attempted to unite actors and events on stage with the audience, German dramatist Bertolt Brecht wanted instead to maintain a distance between the audience and the performance. Brecht believed that audiences should not be led to believe the events of the play were occurring in present time. He thought it was crucial that the audience enjoy the play but avoid relating to the fictional characters in the performance. He also believed that actors should execute their roles without attempting to identify with the character. Brecht attempted to return theatre to the epic form in which a story was retold or narrated rather than enacted. Stage scenery was kept sparse, lighting effects were seldom used, lighting sources were kept visible to the audience and words were cast onto a screen that summarized each part of the play before it began. These devices served to remind the audience of the artificiality of the production.

Auguste character

The auguste character-type is often an anarchist, a joker, or a fool. He is clever and has much lower status than the whiteface. Classically, the whiteface character instructs the auguste character to perform his bidding. The auguste has a hard time performing a given task, which leads to funny situations. Sometimes the auguste plays the role of an anarchist and purposefully has trouble following the whiteface's directions. Sometimes the auguste is confused or is foolish and is screwing up less deliberately.

The contra-auguste:

The contra-auguste plays the role of the mediator between the whiteface character and the auguste character. He has a lower status than the whiteface but a higher status than the auguste. He aspires to be more like the whiteface and often mimics everything the whiteface does to try to gain approval. The contra-auguste character is often instructed by the whiteface to correct the auguste when he is doing something wrong.

Puppets

A puppet is a representational object manipulated by a puppeteer. It is usually but not always a depiction of a human character and is used in a play or a presentation. The puppet undergoes a process of transformation through being animated, and is normally manipulated by one (or sometimes more than one) puppeteer. Some puppets can be moved electronically. Puppets are made of a wide range of materials, depending upon the effect required and the amount of usage intended, and can be extremely complex or very simple in their construction. In contemporary visual or puppet theatre, puppets are often called "performing objects." There are many different varieties of puppets. Puppeteer Anita Sinclair states, "Through puppetry we accept the outrageous, the absurd or even the impossible, and will permit puppets to say and do things no human could. We allow a puppet to talk to us when no one else can get us to speak. We allow a puppet to smile at us even when we have not been introduced. We also allow a puppet to touch us when a person would lose an arm for the same offence." Puppeteer David Logan states, "Puppetry is a highly effective and dynamically creative means of exploring the richness of interpersonal communication. By its very nature, puppetry concentrates on the puppet rather than the puppeteer. This provides a safety zone for the puppeteer and allows for exploration of unlimited themes through a safe and non-threatening environment for communication."

Finger puppet:
A finger puppet is an extremely simple puppet variant that fits onto a single finger. Finger puppets normally have no moving parts and consist primarily of a hollow cylindrical shape to cover the finger. This form of puppet has limited application and is used mainly in pre-schools or kindergartens for storytelling with young children.

Hand or glove puppet:
This is a puppet controlled by one hand that occupies the interior of the puppet. Larger varieties of hand puppets place the puppeteer's hand in just the puppet's head, controlling the mouth and head. The puppet's body then hangs over the entire arm. Other parts of these puppets are usually not much larger than the hand itself. A sock puppet is a particularly simple type of hand puppet made from a sock.

Shadow puppet:
This is a cutout figure held between a source of light and a translucent screen. It is different from other forms of puppetry, as it is two dimensional in form. Shadow puppets can form solid silhouettes or be decorated with various amounts of cutout details. Colour can be introduced into the cutout shapes to provide a different dimension. Javanese shadow puppets are the classic example of this.

Human Carnival puppets
Human Carnival or Body puppets are designed to be part of a large spectacle and are often used in parades and protests. These figures are at least the size of a human and often much larger, requiring one or more performers to move the body and limbs. The appearance and personality of the person inside is not known and is totally irrelevant to the viewer. Puppeteers must never be revealed at performances. These puppets are particularly associated with large-scale entertainment, such as the nightly parades at the various Disney complexes around the world. Big Bird from Sesame Street is a classic example of a Human Carnival or Body Puppet.

Rod puppet:
This variety of puppet is constructed around a central rod secured to the head. A large glove covers the rod and is attached to the neck of the puppet. A rod puppet is controlled by the puppeteer moving the metal rods attached to the hands of the puppet and by turning the central rod secured to the head.

Marionette

This kind of puppet is suspended and controlled by a number of strings, sometimes with a central rod attached to a control bar held from above by the puppeteer. The control bar can be either horizontal or vertical. Basic strings for operation are usually attached to the head, back, hands (to control the arms), and just above the knee (to control the legs). This form of puppetry requires greater manipulative control than a finger, glove or rod puppet.

Masked performance

Throughout the world masks are used for their expressive power as a feature of masked performance. They are a familiar and vivid element in many folk and traditional pageants, ceremonies, rituals and festivals, many of which are of an ancient origin. The mask is often a part of costume that adorns the whole body and represents a tradition important to a particular society of people. Used almost universally, masks maintain their power and mystery both for their wearers and their audience, retaining an important place in the religious and social life of the community. The continued popularity of wearing masks at carnivals, and for children at parties and for festivals such as Halloween are reminders of the enduring power of pretence and play. The mask is also used in theatrical performance. In many cultural traditions, the masked performer is a central concept and is highly valued. In the western tradition it is sometimes considered a stylistic device, which can be traced back to the Greeks and Romans. Ancestors of the modern clown can be traced to the masked characters of the Commedia dell'Arte. In contemporary western theatre the mask is often used alongside puppetry to create a theatre that is essentially visual rather than verbal. Many of its practitioners have been visual artists.

Masks

A mask is an artifact normally worn on the face, typically for protection, concealment, performance or amusement. Masks have been used since antiquity for both ceremonial and practical purposes. They are usually, but not always, worn on the face, although they may also be positioned for effect elsewhere in relation to the wearer's own head.

The word *mask* came via French *masque* and either Italian *maschera* or Spanish *máscara*. The 5000-year-old Sumerian mask of Warka, believed to be the oldest surviving mask, was looted from the Iraqi National Museum in Baghdad and recovered in 2003.

Clowns

Clowns are comic performers, stereotypically characterized by their colored wigs, stylistic makeup, outlandish costumes and unusually large footwear. Clowning, in its most basic form, can be described as one form of drama without a fourth wall. In other words, a clown acknowledges his audience. The clown's humor today is often visual and includes many elements of physical comedy or slapstick humor.
7.

Whiteface clown

It is important to remember that a whiteface character doesn't always wear the classic whiteface makeup. Additionally, a character can wear traditional whiteface makeup and be an auguste character.

Classic appearance: Traditionally, the whiteface clown uses "clown white" makeup to cover his or her entire face and neck with none of the underlying flesh color showing. In the European whiteface makeup, the ears are painted red. Features, in red and black, are delicate. The classic whiteface clown is traditionally costumed far more extravagantly than the other two clown types, sometimes wearing the ruffled collar and pointed hat that typify the stereotypical "clown suit".

Character: The whiteface character-type is often serious, all-knowing (even if not particularly smart), bossy and cocky. He is the ultimate authority figure, serving the role of "straight-man" and setting up situations that can be turned funny.

Character clowns

The character clown adopts an eccentric character of some type, such as a butcher, a baker, a policeman, a housewife or hobo. Prime examples of this type of clown are the circus tramps Otto Griebling and Emmett Kelly. Red Skelton, Harold Lloyd, Buster Keaton and Charlie Chaplin would all fit the definition of a character clown.

The character clown makeup is a comic slant on the standard human face. Their makeup starts with a flesh-toned base and may make use of anything from glasses, moustaches and beards to freckles, warts, big ears or strange haircuts.

Clowns in a circus

In the circus, a clown might perform an additional circus role:

Walk a tightrope, a highwire, a slack rope or a piece of rope on the ground (though in the last case, the predictably unpredictable clown might be just as likely to wrestle around on the ground with it, as if it were a boa constrictor).

Ride a horse, a zebra, a donkey, an elephant, or even an ostrich.

Substitute himself in the role of "lion tamer."

Act as "emcee," from M.C. or Master of Ceremonies, the preferred term for a clown taking on the role of "Ringmaster."

"Sit in" with the orchestra, perhaps in a "pin spot" in the center ring, or from a seat in the audience.

Anything any other circus performer might do. It is not uncommon for an acrobat, a horseback rider, or a lion tamer to secretly stand in for the clown, the "switch" taking place in a brief moment offstage.

American character clown types

The most prevalent character clown in the American circus is the tramp, hobo, or bum clown. There are subtle differences in the American character clown types. They are (in order of class):

- *The Tramp,* who is migratory and finds work where he travels.
- *The Hobo,* also migratory, but does not work where he travels.
- *The Bum,* who is non-migratory and non-working.

History of clowning

Clowning is a form of entertainment that has appeared in some manner in virtually every culture. In most cultures the clown is a ritual character associated with festivals or rites of passage and is often very different from the most popular western form. In Europe, up until as late as the 19th century the clown was a typical everyday character and often appeared in carnivals. The performance is symbolic of liminality. Being outside the rules of regular society, the clown is able to subvert the normal order. This basic premise is contemporarily used by many activists to point out social absurdity. A popular early form of clown was the fool, a role that can be traced back as far as ancient Egypt and appears as the first card in the Tarot deck. Most fools suffered from some physical or mental deformity, and were given to the local landlord as a charge because their families were unable to look after them. The surrounding communities often feared them. They were the butt of jokes and their masters had the power to inflict violence upon them, even taking their lives. However, being perceived 'idiots,' they were often the only people in court who enjoyed free speech, and during the 16th century, especially in France, actors began to train as fools often in order to have the ability to make satirical comment. There is evidence of the 'wise fool,' similar in function to the jester, in many other cultures.

Clowns of this era and eras previous to it were also associated with jugglers, who were seen as pariahs of society alongside actors, prostitutes and lepers, and thus (at least in Europe) wore stripes, or motley - cloth associated with marginalized people such as the condemned, with strong associations with the devil. Jugglers often used clowning techniques, and the later court jesters often danced, performed acrobatics and juggled. During the 16th century the Commedia dell'arte also became a huge influence on perceptions of the clown in Europe, and influence which passed through pantomime, into vaudeville and on to the touring circuses of the 19th and 20th centuries. The Commedia took influences from the grotesque masked clowns of carnivals and mystery plays, and began in market places as a way to sell vegetables. It became incredibly popular throughout Europe amongst both the general public and the courts. The stock characters of the commedia originally included the Zanni - peasant clowns, Pantalone, the old Miser, Il Dottore - The Banal Doctor, and then grew from there to incorporate the Lovers, Arlecchino, Pedrolino, and Brighella, who have survived into the twentieth century in one form or another.

Mime

A mime is an actor who communicates entirely by gesture and facial expression. He mimics or imitates (a person or manner), especially for satirical effect. ("The actor mimicked the President very accurately.") He may also act out with gestures and bodily movements only,

using no words. ("The acting students mimed eating an apple.") A mime gives a performance using gestures and body movements without words.

Reading drama

Despite the inherent problems in reading drama, there are strategies that are useful in developing skills and techniques to enrich the experience.
Read the play through initially at one sitting, then reread it making notes on dominant themes, characters, and difficult passages. Reading without pausing helps give the material a flow that can be missing from drama text. This also helps clarify the major themes and broad outlines of the work.
As plays are written to be spoken aloud, it is a good practice to read them aloud to better capture the verbal cadences and linguistic features not evident in written text. Reading aloud can sometimes give a better sense of a passage and help understand difficult text by placing it into context. The language of drama is keyed to oral production and replicating this is an excellent tool.
Reading in a group is a way to catch the flavor of characters interacting in a drama. One can find a better a sense of how the dialogue functions and therefore the roles of various characters in the play are more easily understood.

Reading dramatic dialogue

Dramatic dialogue can be difficult to interpret and changes depending upon the tone used and which words are emphasized. Where the stresses, or meters, of dramatic dialogue fall can determine meaning. Variations in emphasis are only one factor in the manipulability of dramatic speech. Tone is of equal or greater importance and expresses a range of possible emotions and feelings that cannot be readily discerned from the script of a play. The reader must add tone to the words to understand the full meaning of a passage. Recognizing tone is a cumulative process as the reader begins to understand the characters and situations in the play. Other elements that influence the interpretation of dialogue include the setting, possible reactions of the characters to the speech, and possible gestures or facial expressions of the actor. There are no firm rules to guide the interpretation of dramatic speech. An open and flexible attitude is essential in interpreting dramatic dialogue.

Reading dramatic action

Stage directions: Action is a crucial element in the production of a dramatic work. Many dramas contain little dialogue and much action. In these cases, it is essential for the reader to carefully study stage directions and visualize the action on the stage. Benefits of understanding stage directions include knowing which characters are on the stage at all times, who is speaking to whom, and following these patterns through changes of scene. Stage directions also provide additional information, some of which is not available to a live audience. The nature of the physical space where the action occurs is vital, and stage directions help with this. The historical context of the period is important in understanding what the playwright was working with in terms of theaters and physical space. The type of staging possible for the author is a good guide to the spatial elements of a production.

Advantages of reading drama as text

An oft-heard criticism of reading drama is that the experience pales when compared to watching a performance. There are however some advantages to reading drama as text:

Freedom fpoint of view , and perspective that the written text does not. Text is free of interpretations of actors, directors, producers, and technical staging. Additional information - the text of a drama may be accompanied by notes or prefaces placing the work in a social or historical context. Stage directions may also provide relevant information about the author's purpose. None of this is typically available at live or filmed performances.

Study and understanding - difficult or obscure passages may be studied at leisure and supplemented by explanatory works. This is particularly true of older plays with unfamiliar language which cannot be fully understood without an opportunity to study the material.

Using your imagination

A play is written to be spoken aloud. The drama is in many ways inseparable from performance. Reading drama ideally involves using imagination to visualize and recreate the play with characters and settings. The reader stages the play in his imagination, watching characters interact and developments unfold. Sometimes this involves simulating a theatrical presentation, while some may imagine the events happening before them. In either case, the reader is imagining the unwritten in order to recreate the dramatic experience. Novels present some of the same problems, but a narrator will provide much more information about the setting, characters, inner dialogues and many other supporting details. In drama, much of this is missing and we are required to use our powers of projection and imagination to taste the full flavor of the dramatic work. There are many empty spaces in reading dramatic texts that must be supplied by the reader to fully appreciate the work.

Benefits of theatre program in elementary or secondary schools

Schools that provide theatre programs and classes can benefit students by increasing critical and creative thinking. Theatre programs can help students to develop problem-solving skills as well as help students become effective communicators. Students learn how to collaborate with others and to coordinate their individual skills within a group. They learn planning and implementation skills, as well as how to research using libraries, computers and living sources. Students in theater programs can gain a greater understanding of cultural and historical events and beliefs. These students have the opportunity to develop a high-level of self-awareness as well as to increase self-confidence and become more socially aware.

Incorporating theater in elementary school

First grade
In the first grade, students can be exposed to various forms of theatre. They can gain knowledge of the theatre by viewing formal, informal, video and television productions. The goal is to teach children how to process, analyze and respond to sensory information that is unique to theatre. First grade students can be taught the skills of artistic perception through lessons involving basic comprehension of theatre and its vocabulary. Creative expression can be cultivated by performing improvisational and pantomime activities. These students may also dramatize fictional and real-life stories to demonstrate a plot structure

containing a beginning, middle and end. They can learn to identify the history and culture of theatre by understanding the geographical origins of a story. In first grade, students should be allowed to develop aesthetic judgment by expressing their emotional reactions to various forms of theatre.

Second grade
Students should be taught about artistic perception through activities and lessons that utilize theatre vocabulary. Students should have the opportunity to demonstrate an understanding of artistic perception by acting out alternative endings to stories. Second grade students should be taught creative expression through activities that allow them to perform in groups to build cooperation skills. They can be taught how to pantomime concepts like hunger, anger, friendship and excitement. With regards to theatre history and context, students can be taught to identify stories from different cultures as well as identify universal character-types. Aesthetic judgment can be developed by allowing students to recognize and critique an actor's performance with regard to the actor's use of voice, movement and gesture. By second grade, students should have the ability to identify the moral of a story.

Third grade
In third grade, students are further exposed to artistic perception through lessons on theatre vocabulary. They should also be taught to identify the five basic elements of a story: who, what, where, when and why (the "Five Ws"). Creative expression can be developed by allowing students to work together to write a script that uses the Five Ws. They should also be able to demonstrate knowledge of stage direction by writing a script that uses basic blocking. Historical aspects of theatre can be taught by allowing students to perform different

- 14 -

versions of similar stories from around the world. Students in the third grade should be able to identify universal themes in stories and can be taught aesthetic judgment by developing and applying criteria to judge the success or quality of a performance. These students should also be able to compare the content and messages contained in two separate works.

Fourth grade
Students in the fourth grade should continue expanding their theatre vocabulary. They should also build upon their existing knowledge of artistic perspective by learning to identify a character's motives. Students should learn how subtle changes in voice can be used to convey meaning during speaking and acting. The use of artistic expression should be cultivated by participation in activities where the students must express the emotions of actors through use of gestures. They should also retell stories in various tones, including comic and tragic. Students should have the opportunity to create a character through use of costumes, masks and props. Regarding the history of theatre, students should be introduced to local theatre history and trends. Their aesthetic judgment abilities should be developed by critiquing performances based on the elements of acting they have studied. They should also understand the audience's impact on various types of performances. Fourth grade students should be able to view a dramatic performance and identify the methods employed by the scriptwriter to evoke a certain response from the audience.

Fifth grade
Students in the fifth grade should develop artistic perception through the use of theatrical vocabulary in descriptions of theatrical experiences. The students should be taught to identify the structural elements of plot in scripts and performances. This includes exposition, complication, crisis, climax and resolution. Students should be allowed to develop their creative expression abilities through participation in improvisational activities examining universal themes. Students should also understand the concepts of blocking in theatre. The students should be further allowed to develop their creativity by participating in an actual performance where they perform the duties of an actor, director, writer or technical assistant. In regards to teaching the historical and cultural aspects of theatre, students should be allowed to make costumes, sets and props for a cultural celebration. Students should also examine cultural traditions and beliefs as they are reflected in the stories and plays of various cultures. In regards to the aesthetic element, students should evaluate the methods used by actors to convey meaning in their performances.

Incorporating theater in secondary schools

Sixth grade
Students in the sixth grade should continue to learn and to use theatre vocabulary. Artistic perception is taught through lessons that involve the importance of production value. Creative expression can be developed by having students participate in performances that demonstrate their knowledge of text, context and subtext. Students should utilize facial expression, voice, gestures and timing in a performance to convey the essence of the character they are playing. Creativity can be further developed by having students write a play that uses monologues, dialogues, actions,

settings and a multitude of characters. Students should be asked to create a script that demonstrates their knowledge of a specific culture or historical period. They should also study theatrical traditions and histories on a global level. Sixth grade students should be able to aesthetically judge a theatrical experience by taking into consideration the quality and effectiveness of lighting, sets, costume, makeup and props. Students should also understand how theatre, television, film, politics and culture can interact and influence each other.

Seventh grade
Students in the seventh grade should be introduced to more theatre vocabulary. They should develop the ability to identify dramatic elements including foreshadowing, crisis, rising action, catharsis and denouement. In order to develop skills in creative expression students should be allowed to explore character and motivation by participating in rehearsals. They should learn the value of maintaining a rehearsal script in order to organize their rehearsal time and to keep track of their thoughts and ideas concerning blocking, props and lighting. Students should be taught to incorporate tension and suspense into their writing. Regarding the historical and cultural aspects of theatre, student should participate in a culture-specific performance where they design and create the masks, costumes and sets. Students should also be able to compare and contrast various theatrical styles. With regard to aesthetic judgment, students should understand how cultural influences affect the content and meaning of drama.

Eighth grade:
In the eighth grade students should continue to develop theatre vocabulary. They should learn to identify recurring themes, such as loyalty and revenge, in scripts and performances. Students

should explore the use of figurative language and imagery in various dramatic works. With regard to creative expression, students should create short performances that target a specific genre or style of theatre, such as vaudeville and melodrama. Students should also participate in improvisational activities in which they use voice, blocking, monologue and pantomime to covey meaning in their character. Students should understand how American history is and was reflected in various styles of theatre, such as minstrel shows and musicals. Students should also be able to identify how technology has changed theatre over time. In order to develop skills in aesthetic judgment, students should write a full review of a dramatic production. They should also be able to identify similar plots and themes occurring in differing theatrical styles and cultures.

Theatre curriculum in secondary education

Teaching theatre in schools is often seen as unnecessary and disruptive to the educational curriculum, but studies have shown that theatre classes can offer many benefits to students. Theatre classes help to develop emotional intelligence, an everyday skill that is crucial in developing relationships and making life choices. Schools that neglect to incorporate a theatre component in the curriculum risk sending some of their students into the world not fully equipped with the emotional intelligence they will need in life. Author Reed Larson's study, published in the journal *Child Development*, explains that through a study conducted in an Illinois high school he observed that students who were taking a theatre class had much more positive emotional experiences than those who were not taking a theatre class. Larson believes that theatre class helps students learn how to constructively work through emotions rather than to react negatively in stressful or frustrating situations. Additionally, the theatre students in Larson's study were described as better able to help other students master a higher degree of emotional intelligence.

Course description
Students in high school theatre arts courses will study, write, research, critique, create, design, perform and participate in a variety of theatre-based learning experiences. Three levels of instruction will be included, allowing for a total of four years of theatre arts classes. The courses will include instruction in performance and design techniques, style, historical motifs and genres, creating performance-based experiences while using appropriate technology and media. These courses will develop critical thinking, creativity and aesthetic perception and will reinforce skills in leadership and collaboration. The program of study will generate a heightened sensitivity to the arts and will explore theatre's significance and influence on society.

Applying theater lessons to other subject areas

In first grade students learn to cooperate in group activities. They also begin to understand the concept that, like a story, all things in life have a beginning, middle and an end. In second grade students learn problem-solving skills, which can be carried into other courses. By the third grade, students learn to question events and gain information through applying the five Ws (who, what, when, where and why). In fourth grade students learn to use acting as a tool to understand local history. They also learn to identify with a team in order to accomplish a specific goal. In fifth grade students learn about the various career options available to professional actors and theatrical

technicians. In sixth grade student learn how theatrical skills are used in social sciences, such as advertising and marketing and in seventh grade they learn how voice can be used to project confidence during oral presentations. In eighth grade students begin to understand the various jobs available in theatre and they learn to research the educational requirements necessary for those jobs.

Relationship between art, music, and literature
Art and music contain many opportunities for interacting with literature for the enrichment of all. Students could apply their knowledge of art and music by creating illustrations for a work, or creating a musical score for a text. Students could discuss the meanings of texts and decide on their illustrations, or a score could amplify the meaning of the text. Understanding the art and music of a period can make the experience of literature a richer, more rewarding experience. Students should be encouraged to use the knowledge of art and music to illuminate the text. Examining examples of dress, architecture, music, and dance of a period may be helpful in a fuller engagement of the text. Much of period literature lends itself to the analysis of the prevailing taste in art and music of an era, which helps place the literary work in a more meaningful context.

Trade books
Some educators say stories about heroes serve as a source for teaching values. Some studies indicate recent trends on teaching values in connection with methods of analysis. Personal models such as heroes in history, fiction, and current events help to exemplify and encourage emulation of certain virtues or desirable traits of character such as civility, courage, honesty, perseverance, self-restraint, compassion, and fairness,

as well as respect for the dignity of individuals and responsibility for the common good. Trade books are a good source for using heroes to teach values. These stories should be accurate and present both positive and negative aspect of a person's life. Multimedia instruction, including the use of videotapes, can help add depth to the portrayal.

Children's literature
Children's literature is designed to be read and enjoyed primarily by young readers. Early children's literature was written exclusively for educational purposes. Beginning in the middle of the 18th century, children's books were written to entertain as well as edify. Adventure stories for boys became popular in the 19th century, as did fiction designed for girls, such as Louisa May Alcott's "Little Women" (1868), and Johanna Spyri's " Heidi" (1880). Mark Twain and Robert Louis Stevenson became important writers of children's fiction during this time.

Recent years have emphasized more realism in children's literature. Opposed to the traditional view of shielding children from the realities of life, many now advocate books that are not only realistic but tragic, providing an opportunity for catharsis for young readers. An example of this type of fiction is William Armstrong's "Sounder" (1969), a novel of the evils of a segregated society written for young readers.

Teaching character acting

The objective of a unit on character acting is to teach students how to develop, communicate and sustain characters in various performances. Students should learn to use sensory perception and emotional recall as tools to interpret and enact characters. They should learn how to recognize differences in characters and how to use their imaginations to create

and show the thoughts and emotions of a character. Students should learn how characters can be used to develop situations in both individual and collaborative works. Students should develop skills in acting analysis as well as become familiar with improvisational skills. Students should be taught how to use vocal techniques in character portrayal and how to use movement to convey a character's thoughts and feelings. Character acting units should also include lessons on how technical elements of theatre can be used to enhance characterizations.

Gauging students' progress
Beginning level: At a beginner's level, students should be capable of using physical, emotional and social elements to portray a character in monologues, duets and improvised scenes. They should be capable of recreating a character through observation. Beginning students should have the ability to use their imaginations to improvise a character's thoughts and emotions and should be able to use improvisational skills to create a character. Students should be able to demonstrate an understanding of how vocal techniques are used to control volume and clarity when speaking. They should be able to distinguish between the various styles of acting as well as to identify ways to analyze characters. Beginning students should have an understanding of how technical elements like costume, makeup, props and lighting can enhance character development. Beginning students should be able to demonstrate through improvised scenes how movement can be used to express the thoughts and emotions of characters.

Intermediate level: Intermediate-level students should be capable of incorporating physical, emotional and social elements into their portrayal of individual characters. They should be able to create characters based on analysis of a

- 18 -

script and to develop characters from the thoughts and feelings expressed in script dialogue. Students should have the ability to use improvisational skills when acting. Intermediate students should also have the ability to use analytical skills to develop characters in scripted scenes and to use movement to express thoughts and feelings in scripted scenes. Students should have the ability to use various styles of acting to portray characters. Intermediate students should be able to incorporate technical elements like costume, makeup, props and lighting to enhance characters.

Advanced level: Advanced students should be able to develop, communicate and sustain a character for the duration of a published script. They should have an ability to incorporate physical, social and emotional elements while portraying characters. The advanced student can create characterizations using complete scripts and can use imagination to develop a character's thoughts and emotions based on the dialogue and relationships within the script. Advanced students can use improvisational skills to create complex characters. They should be able to develop and analyze various approaches to characterizations and to determine the effectiveness of certain approaches as they are used in full-length scripts. Advanced students should show proficiency in selecting and applying technical elements to specific characters in full-length productions. They should be capable of using the vocal techniques implied in a script. Advanced students should have the ability to perform in ensembles while utilizing movement to convey thoughts, feelings and character.

Teaching script analysis

In a basic unit on script analysis geared toward 9th-12th grade students, the lessons should teach students how to improvise, write and edit scripts. The students should learn the principles of

script writing and must be taught how to examine their own life experiences as well as how to create imaginary situations that can then be used in script writing. Students should be instructed as to how to use proper vocabulary involving meaning, character and subtext when writing a script. Students should have an understanding of the technical elements of theatre when writing a script. A unit on script analysis should also contain instruction on methods of developing and resolving dramatic problems. Upon completion, students should be able to demonstrate a basic understanding of people and life situations and how these can be used in a script.

Gauging students' progress
At the most basic level, a student who studies script writing should be capable of writing alone or with others. A student should be able to write original scenarios as well as create various characters, incorporating the appropriate literary elements and devices into the writing. The student should be able to identify dramatic situations, stage directions, technical notations and colloquial dialogues or subtext in published literature. In addition to being able to use the knowledge from the beginning level, the intermediate level student must be able to create multiple characters and settings and incorporate them into a complete scene containing a clear beginning, middle and end. Intermediate students should be capable of using colloquial dialogue and including stage directions and technical notations in their own writing. Advanced students should be able to create complex characters. They should have the ability to create a script in the appropriate format, which contains dynamic and dramatic situations, plot and development, colloquial dialogue and subtext and well-developed characters.

Teaching stage direction

When introducing students to theatre, it is important to provide them with the proper vocabulary tools. For example, students could be placed in groups of three to five and instructed to draw or sketch a stage set and then describe in writing the set they create. This written description would allow students to utilize any existing knowledge they have of stage direction while discovering the difficulty of conveying stage descriptions without the proper terminology. Once the activity is completed, the proper vocabulary terms are introduced. These include upstage, downstage, stage right, stage left and center stage, which are then explained in relation to how they are used in scripts and by actors and directors. This activity can be brought to life by using the classroom as a stage and having students move to the area that matches the name they call out. This lesson can be taken to a higher level by providing scripts in which the stage directions have been omitted and instructing students to provide their own stage direction based on the actions in the play.

Teaching scene design

It is important for theatre students to understand the importance of scene design in both formal and informal productions. Students should learn to conceptually design and technically produce scene design through various exercises and projects. Lessons involving scene design should cover the terminology, techniques and materials used in theatre performances. The students should gain an understanding of the various roles in theatre management. Lessons should examine theatre design and teach students how to analyze scene design in various types of productions. Lessons should explore scene design as a profession while including activities that allow students to actively participate in the development and production of scene design. Students should be given the opportunity to participate in scene design in order to determine their aptitude and inclination to pursue this particular niche in the future.

Gauging students' progress

Beginning level: Students who have taken only one theatre class are considered beginners. After completing a unit on scene design, beginning students should be able to identify both the technical and managerial elements involved in creating theatrical and dramatic effects for performances. They should be able to demonstrate their knowledge by taking on various roles or responsibilities in a dramatic performance. Students should understand the roles and responsibilities involved in theatre management including box office, advertising and house management. Beginning students should be able to demonstrate their knowledge of scene design, costume, sound, lighting and props. They should also understand and be able to demonstrate their knowledge of scene design as a profession and a hobby.

Intermediate level: Intermediate-level theatre students will have had two to three years of theatre classes. They should have the ability to create technical designs as well as theatre management designs. Intermediate students should have the ability to collaborate with a group to perform various technical and managerial roles and responsibilities. Students at this level should have the ability to apply their knowledge by participating in tasks involved with advertising, house management and box office duties. At this level, students should participate in various design positions in a theatre performance and should be able to distinguish between the possibility of pursuing theatre scene design as a hobby or as a profession.

Advanced level: Advance students have taken three or four years of theatre classes. Advanced students should be able to apply their knowledge by creating technical and theatre management designs for full-length dramatic productions. Advanced students should be capable of managing and supervising a technical crew or staff. They should be capable of demonstrating leadership abilities by organizing and overseeing a staff that is responsible for the various tasks involved in theatre management. Advanced students must be able to analyze, design and execute the requirements for any given design element in any type of production. Advanced students should actively participate in various theatre positions in order to assess their own aptitude and inclination to pursue those roles in either a professional or a vocational capacity.

Teaching directing

During a unit on theatrical directing, students should learn to interpret scripts, conduct rehearsals and organize theatre productions. Students should receive instruction on how to analyze a dramatic text to determine production value. They should learn how to solve acting and technical problems as well as how to evaluate the suitability of various solutions. Lessons should provide students the opportunity to develop leadership skills through directing both formal and informal productions. Students should also have the chance to develop collaborative skills by working in groups to direct and produce performances. The functions and responsibilities of directors should be covered in the lessons. Students should also gain an understanding of the principles and importance of stage movement.

Gauging students' progress
Beginning level: Students at a beginning level should be familiar with the role of a director and be able to identify a

director's responsibilities. Students should be capable of working alone or in groups to demonstrate the leadership and collaborative skills used by a director when creating a production. Students should be able to read a script, identifying potential problems that a director might face and should be able to propose solutions to those problems. Students should be capable of demonstrating their knowledge of stage movement, including blocking and choreography. Students at a beginning level should also be familiar with the historical timelines and trends related to directing.

Intermediate and advanced levels: Students who have taken two to three years of theatre classes are considered to be at the intermediate level. These students should be capable of performing the role of a director in a short scene. They should be able to work alone and in a group, easily conveying leadership and collaborative skills through directing short productions and one-act performances. Once intermediate students have directed a short or one-act piece, they should be able to identify problems in the directing process and creatively find solutions to those problems. Intermediate students should demonstrate the ability to incorporate the appropriate stage movement in a scene that they are directing. Advanced students who have taken theatre for three or four years should be able to fully direct an ensemble performance while integrating the proper stage movement into the performance. They should also be capable of anticipating problems and be able to quickly resolve unforeseen problems that might arise while directing.

Teaching history of theatre

During a unit on the history of theatre, students should learn to research and evaluate the origins of theatre. They should learn to recognize the characteristics of various genres, eras and styles of theatre. They should be able to understand and discuss the contributions made to theatre by historical figures in each era and theatre style. Students should grasp how the culture, religion and politics of each geographical area affected the development of theatre and have an understanding of the social impact that theatre itself has made. They should be able to recognize and name the works and authors that dominated each genre and era of theatre. Students should also be able to discuss significant figures in the history of theatre and the contributions they made in the areas of acting, scene design, script analysis, lighting, sound, special effects, directing and theatrical management.

Teaching theatrical presentation

Theatrical presentation should involve familiarizing students with the broad range of activities that can be considered theatrical forms, which include music, dance, performance and visual arts. Students should examine the structure of dramatic productions and understand how that structure is the underlying form of all arts. They should be able to create a performance that integrates knowledge of various forms of theatre. Lessons should provide a means for students to study both traditional and non-traditional methods of artistic production. This should include hands-on experience in emerging technology in theatrical productions including film, video and computer.

Teaching scene comprehension

Theatre students should receive formal instruction on scene comprehension. Scene comprehension consists of the ability to analyze, critique, and infer meaning from various theatrical productions. Students should be exposed to several productions including both

formal and informal performances. Students can exercise comprehension by viewing musical performances, dramatic productions, television and film. By critiquing these performances, students can gain an understanding of how to interpret and analyze productions, as well as understand the role played by the audience. Students should learn how the audience can be incorporated into various types of productions and should be introduced to methods of judging the aesthetic quality of a performance. They should learn to compare and contrast various performances in order to analyze the effectiveness of delivery.

Indicators of proficient students
Proficient students can use theatre vocabulary to describe theatrical experiences. They are able to collaborate with other theatre students and participate in a theatrical production in any related capacity. Students are able to recognize subtext, symbolism and metaphors in scripts and performances. Creatively, proficient students are able to create characters using script analysis, research and imagination. They can also utilize their knowledge to make acting decisions during rehearsals. Students can write dialogue and scenes that employ dramatic structure and should be able to design, produce and perform plays that demonstrate their comprehension of various theatrical styles and historical periods.

Indicators of advanced students
Advanced students should demonstrate the ability to creatively develop characters from a variety of dramatic texts, both realistic and fictional. They should have the skills to research, reflect and revise their acting choices for various characters. Advanced students should be able to use dialogue to advance action when writing a script. They should also be able to utilize the basic dramatic structure while writing a script and to

- 22 -

develop complex characters to populate the script. In regards to understanding the historical aspects of theatre, advanced students should be able to research and perform a particular historical or cultural piece while using the appropriate dialect and mannerisms throughout the performance. Advanced students should understand the way the impact that theatre has and continues to have on society and culture. Students should also be capable of designing, performing and directing plays that are representational of specific theatrical styles. Advanced students should be able to use the appropriate vocabulary terms to discuss their aesthetic judgments of dramatic works.

Important terms

Dramatic performance terms
Acting process: this term refers to the methods and materials from which an actor draws the ability to perform. Actors should be able to verbalize the tools they use in their acting processes.
Affective memory-a technique in which an actor reactivates a past experience to gain the emotional and psychological feelings associated with those events and then transfer them to a performance; used when the actor believes the character they are portraying is undergoing an event that emotionally parallels that which the actor has experienced in real life.

Atmosphere-defined by Michael Chekhov as the inherent energy within a specific place. Actors may imagine they are in a specific location while performing in order to depict the corresponding emotions and actions that would best suit that environment, thus creating an atmosphere.

Character acting occurs when an actor must make a change to their physical person in order to perform a role. This may include the use of dialect or accents that are not part of the actor's real persona or using stage makeup to create a specific facial disfigurement.

Acting terms
Articulation: the ability to clearly pronounce words while acting or performing.
Blocking: the development of the movements of actors on stage in relation to other actors and scenery/props.
Catharsis: the purging of an emotion, such as fear or grief, which can occur while performing on stage.
Concentration: the ability of an actor to be "in character" through use of dialogue, attitude, voice, costume, expressions and mannerisms.
Cold reading: reading a script for the first time.
Context: the conditions or climate in which a play was written or meant to be performed.
Cue: signal that serves as an indicator of another action that is about to occur.
Denouement occurs when the final conflict in a production is resolved.
Diction is the choice of words that actors use to express themselves.
Downstage is the physical location on the stage that is closest to the audience.
Emotional memory is a tool used by actors in which they use their own specific memories of events in which they reacted emotionally to understand the emotions of the character they are portraying.
A *dramaturg* is a specialist in theatre who may be called upon to advise actors, directors and producers in certain aspects of theatrical productions.
Exposition occurs when one must provide information regarding the facts of the plot, usually to the audience either before or during a performance.
Level is the height of an actor's head in a performance while carrying out certain actions.

Stages

- 23 -

Most simply, a stage is the space where a dramatic production takes place. There are currently three major types of stages in use:

Theatre in the round or the arena stage allows the audience to surround the stage, which provides a much different dramatic experience for both players and audiences alike. Originally, this form of stage was used in classical theatre in Greece and Rome, and is widely used today in smaller experimental theaters around the world.

The apron or thrust stage seats audiences on the sides of a platform. Less commonly used today, Shakespeare's Globe Theatre was an early form of the apron stage.

The most common stage in current use is the proscenium stage where the audience sits in front of a stage framed by the acting space. This form is very common in drama, opera, and musical presentations.

The type of stage used affects the action of the dramatic work, and each offers a unique experience to the audience.

Stage areas
↔Backstage area↔

Stage Right	Up Stage Center	Stage Left
Center Stage Right	Center Stage	Center Stage Left
Down Stage Right	Down Stage Center	Down Stage Left

↔Audience seating↔

Set design

Tools for modeling
Modern set designers are able to utilize a variety of modeling software to create set designs and layouts, but design software can be costly and difficult to learn. More primitive methods that are still very common include *renderings*. A rendering is a free-hand drawing of a set based on the first impressions of the designer or director. The renderings rarely ever represent a complete idea and are changed throughout preproduction. Designers may also create a set using a ground plan, which is a drawing of the set design from above the stage looking directly down. This allows the designer to gauge the space between items on the stage. Set designers may also use three-dimensional models and thumbnail sketches. Scale drawings of the set are called *elevations* and are commonly used in set design.

Mise-en-scene
Mise-en-scene is a French term that translates as "put in the scene." The term refers to everything that is placed upon a stage to be filmed or shown as part of a performance. The term can refer to actors, scenery, lighting and costumes. It can refer to the manner in which the performance space is utilized or to the movements of the actors in relation to the scenery. It is a very all-encompassing term. Scholars agree that the term can take on various meanings and some feel that mise-en-scene is better defined as the emotional tone of a film.

Technical aspects of theatre

Apron: the section of a stage that projects into the auditorium.
  Aria: solo performance in an opera that conveys the emotional state of the main character.
Array: the loudspeakers that are used in a performance.

- 24 -

Artic: an articulated lorry used to transport sets, costumes, props and technical equipment between venues.

An **aside** occurs when an actor speaks directly to the audience, though the other characters are not privy to the information being shared.

ASM is an acronym for Assistant Stage Manager.

Attribute: the parameters of moving light that can be controlled, such as pan, tilt and gobos.

Avista: scene changes that are done in view of the audience.

Backing: either the piece of scenery that hides the technical areas or the money that is invested in a commercial production.

Backlight: light that comes from upstage or behind the actors.

Baffle: material that is used to prevent light from spilling over from one area into another. It may also refer to a panel used in an auditorium to reduce the reflection of sound.

Ballyhoo: the lighting effect produced when swinging a spot beam in a figure eight pattern.

Barndoors: hinged metal flaps that are attached to the front of Fresnel spotlights, which can be opened or closed to control the light beam.

Bastard prompt: used in situations where the prompt corner must be stage right instead of stage left.

Battens: floodlights set up in compartments allowing the mixing of light colors.

Beamlight: a flood lantern that uses a parabolic reflector to create a high-intensity parallel beam.

Beginners term shouted by stage management to signify it is time for the actors who appear in the first scene to come onto the stage.

Bell board: a live sound effects board that can play sound effects such as doorbells, ringing phones and sirens.

Bifocal spot: a profile light that contains two sets of shutters. One set produces a hard-edged light; the other, a soft-edged light.

Birdie: a low-volt light that can be used as uplighting or to conceal set pieces.

Bit part: a very small role in a performance.

Black box: a studio theatre, usually surrounded by black curtains, in which the audience and actors share space.

Black hole: a part of the stage that was left unlit intentionally or accidentally.

Blacks: the clothing worn by stage management to visually minimize their presence on stage, or the drapes affixed to the set to hide technical equipment.

Bleed through: when lighting is slowly cross-faded from a scene occurring downstage to one occurring upstage; the two scenes are separated by a piece of gauze which can be lit to appear either opaque or invisible.

Bleeding: when dimmers are not trimmed correctly, allowing the lantern to glow even when the dimmer control is at a minimum.

Blinders: lamps that are set up around a stage facing the audience to prevent them from seeing backstage.

Blues: used backstage as working lights; usually remain on even when blackouts occur to help actors and technicians see what they are doing.

Book: may refer to a prompt book or to the unsung parts of a musical.

Book flat: free standing piece of scenery that can be folded in half for quick scene changes.

Boom-arm: mechanical structure which is mounted on a microphone to facilitate movement.

Border: a piece of cloth used to mask lighting rigs or flown scenery from the audience.

Boss plate: metal plate in stage floor that is used to bolt down scenery.

Breakaway: a prop or a part of the set that is made to break upon impact.

Breakup: abstract Gobo* that is used to provide a textured light with no distinctive pattern.

Bump: sudden flash of light often used as a cue.

Burnout: a colored gel that has lost its color or has melted with use.

Call: a request that an actor come to stage to prepare for entrance into a scene.

Calling the show: giving verbal cues to lighting-, sound- and fly- operators, as well as stage crew throughout a performance.

Cans: headsets, earpieces and headphones used to communicate between technical departments.

Catharsis- occurs at the emotional climax of the play when the characters and the audience can achieve emotional cleansing.

CL: the imaginary centerline running down the middle of the stage.

Chain pocket-tab: pocket sewed into the bottom of a cloth to weigh the cloth down.

Chase: repetitious sequence in which the lighting state is changed.

Cheat: an actor's movement without the audience's knowledge.

Check: refers to a smooth decrease in the level of light or sound.

CID, *compact iodide daylight*: a light with a high-intensity lamp that simulates the look of daylight.

Cleaners: lights that are turned on in order to clean and set up a theatre venue.

Clearance: message to stage management from house manager to let them know that the house is ready for the performance to begin.

Clipping: occurs when sound is distorted due to the amp's inability to handle the level of signal.

Back cloth: fabric hung at rear of scene.

Floorcloth fabric designating the acting area or a part of a set.

Frontcloth fabric hung downstage to hide scene changes.

Starcloth: usually black fabric with several small lamps sewn on to give the effect of a starry sky.

CMY: refers to the colors cyan, yellow and magenta, which are used to mix colors in moving lights.

Color call: the list that specifies all of the colors that will be needed for a specific lighting plan.

Color filter: piece of colored plastic that blocks passing of the light of any color but its own.

Additive color: occurs when two beams of different colors are focused onto the same area.

Subtractive color: occurs when two colors of gels are placed in front of a lantern.

Color temperature: refers to warmness or coolness of lighting; high-color temperature lights appear whiter or *cool*.

Come down: refers to the closing time of a show.

Crash box: sealed metal box that contains glass or other breakable items that is thrown backstage to produce the sound of items being broken onstage.

Cross fade: occurs when one lighting effect is brought up to replace the current lighting effect.

Crossover: the path an actor takes from one side of the stage to the other.

CSI, *compact source iodide*: light used in followspots.

Cue light: the system of giving actors and other staff cues by light.

Curtain line: either the imaginary line across the stage where the curtain would be if it were closed or to the final spoken line in a play.

Curtain speech: refers to a speech given by a director or theatre owner before a performance begins.

Denouement: the moments in a performance when the point of the plot is revealed or explained.

Dark: term used when referring to a venue that has been closed either permanently or temporarily between productions.

Dead: adjective describing an article of equipment or scenery that is no longer being used.

Dead room: a room that dulls sound because of its thick sound absorbers.

Dialect coach: specialist brought in to assist actors with specific accents necessary for conversations within the production.

DLC, *digital light curtain*: a remote-controlled batten with color changers.

Dim out: when lighting is reduced, but not completely blocked out, during scene changes.

Dip: multiple meanings; small hidden trap door at stage level which contains electrical outlets; clear lacquer used to tint bulbs for lighting; lighting equipment that is set up at stage level.

Distortion: occurs when sound equipment is overloaded.

Donut: refers to a metal plate with a center hole that can be inserted into lanterns to sharpen focus.

Door flat: a moveable wall with a working door that is used for scenery.

Douser: metal flag that can be moved to block a beam of light in order to eliminate the need to cut off electricity.

Dry run: a technical rehearsal that usually does not involve actors.

ERS: ellipsoidal reflector spotlight.

Effects projector: a lantern that can project images such as clouds or rain.

Animation disc: metal disc with slots that can be rotated in front of a lantern to give the effect of movement in the light.

Exposition: background information on the characters or the plot of the play, usually occurring at the beginning of the play.

FBO: fade to blackout.

Fade: gradual increase or decrease in the level of light or sound

False perspective: design technique that makes the set appear larger than it really is.

False proscenium: a canvas or flat panel placed onto a proscenium stage in order to decrease the size of the space to accommodate a small set.

False stage: a stage floor laid for a production in which scenery may need to be moved from beneath the stage or in order to accommodate a revolving set.

Fill light: light used to compensate for the shadows created by key lighting.

Fills: speakers used in addition to the main sound system to project sound into certain areas.

Fireplace flat: a flat piece of scenery that contains a fireplace.

Fit up: the initial assembly of stage hardware for a production, including setting up scenery.

Flagging: waving one's hand in and out of a beam of light in order to determine where it is focused on stage.

Flipper: a narrow flat of scenery that is attached by a hinge to a wider flat.

Focus chart: the record created by the lighting designer that reveals the exact focus of each lantern in a rig.

FOH: front of house.

Forced perspective: design technique that can be used to make items look larger or smaller by placing them at certain spots on the stage.

Forestage: part of a stage that projects outward into the auditorium.

Found space: a theatre space suitable for performances but not originally designed to be a theatre.

Fourth wall: the imaginary wall that separates the audience and actors.

Haas effect: psychoacoustic phenomenon, produced through experimentation with sound, which produces a 10-15 millisecond delay in sound, which allows the audience to remain focused on the actors and not become distracted by the delayed sound.

Hitting your mark: term used when an actor is standing in the correct spot according to the stage lighting.

Hot spot: the brightest part of a light beam; certain lanterns have controls to eliminate hot spots.

House: can refer to the theatre auditorium or to the audience in the theatre.

House lights: lights used in the auditorium, though they are not part of the actual play.

House manager: member of the theatre staff who is responsible for ensuring the health and safety of audience members during a performance.

IATSE, International Alliance of Theatrical Stage Employees: the union for stage employees.

In the round: a theatre layout in which the acting stage is entirely encircled by audience seating.

Inset: a small set that is arranged inside of a larger set.

Interval: a 15-20 minute break between sections of a performance.

Intonation: the emphasis of certain words during any oral recitation.

Iris: the aperture device placed in a profile lantern to change the size of the light beam; common in followspots.

Key light: the dominant source of light for a performance, the direction of which can change as the play progresses in order to simulate, for example, the rising and setting of the sun.

Kicker lights: refers to lights that flank actors; can be used to enhance the three-dimensional look of things on stage.

Lamp tray: part of a lantern upon which the lamp holder is set; can be hinged, removable or fixed.

Lantern: This term is used very loosely to refer to any unit of light equipment.

Limelight: a type of light no longer used but the term has been adapted into slang for being famous, "in the limelight."

Low smoke: an effect produced when smoke is made to lie close to the floor; can be produced by chilling the smoke as it comes from smoke machine.

Luminaire: term used to refer to any type of lighting equipment.

Lux: the level of illumination appearing on a surface.

Marking out: applying tape to the stage floor during rehearsal to identify the space upon which scenery will later be placed.

Maroon: a pyrotechnic device that can create a loud explosive sound.

Masking: material, neutral in color and used both to define a performance area and to hide technical areas.

Moon box: gives the effect of a rising moon by using a shallow round box with low-wattage lamps covered by thin cloth.

Naturalism: approach to lighting that requires lanterns be placed according to where light would occur in nature.

Neutral density filter: light filter that can be used to decrease the intensity of light without altering its color.

Noise gate: used to decrease background noise, maintaining a specific sound level by muting or increasing a signal in response to the noise level.

OP: *opposite prompt*: refers to the side of the stage opposite of the side from which prompts are received.

On the book: term used to refer to an actor who must use a script during a scene.

Opening the house: when stage management alerts the FOH staff that the stage is set and the audience can begin taking their seats.

Overlay: the wider spot when there are two followspots on the same performer.

Papering the house: a marketing technique in which tickets are given away to make a show seem to be selling better than it actually is.

Parcan: lantern that can produce an intense beam of light; ideal for special effects.

Pass door: door that is located in the wall of the proscenium arch, which acts as a passage between the auditorium and stage.

Passarelle: walkway that allows actors to get close to audience via a path beyond the proscenium arch into the orchestra pit.

Pearl-lamp with a frosted finish that serves to diffuse light; used when soft light is needed.

Perches-lighting platforms located on sides of a stage behind the proscenium.

Pin spot-luminaire used to focus a small tight beam of light onto a specific spot.

Pit-refers to the area of a theatre in which the orchestra is seated.

Pit net: net placed over the pit area of the theatre to prevent actors and objects from falling into the area where the orchestra is be located.

Places: a term called out by directors when it is time for actors to stand in their appropriate positions to begin a scene.

Platform stage: usually refers to an acting stage that is lifted from the floor in a space that was not created as a theatre.

Preproduction: refers to the time before a production in which the planning is done.

Preview: performances that occur prior to opening night.

Principals: refers to the main actors in a production.

Promenade: a theatrical arrangement in which the audience moves around the acting area to see the performance from multiple locations.

Prompt book: master copy of a script that details all of the actors' movements and technical cues; usually maintained by stage management.

Prompt: side-generally refers to the left side of the stage or whichever side the prompt corner is located.

Prompter: theatre's staff member who follows the script as the play is performed, standing ready to remind an actor of a line in the event they forget during a performance.

Proscenium arch-refers to the frame through which the audience sees a performance; usually the wall opening between the stage and auditorium.

Quarter: a term that stage management shouts to actors backstage when the show will start in fifteen minutes.

Half: a term that stage management shouts to actors backstage when the show will begin in thirty minutes.

Quick change: costume change that must happen so quickly that it must be done near the side of the stage instead of completely backstage.

Raked auditorium: refers to audience seating that is arranged in a forward sloping manner.

Raked stage: refers to a stage that slopes upwards towards the upstage or back end.

Receiving house: venue that hosts incoming touring companies.

Repertoire: theatrical company organization in which two or more productions are alternated throughout the performing season.

Reprise: term used in musicals to refer to the repetition of a song or dance at a later point in the show.

Rider: information sent to a venue by a theatrical company providing a detailed list of all of the technical requirements needed for a performance.

Run: refers to the number of times a production is scheduled to show.

Scene shop: section of the theatre where technicians and designers construct scenery.

Scoop: lamp mounted in a large ellipsoidal reflector; usually produces

- 29 -

soft-edged circular beam of light and is used as a floodlight.

Scrim: coarse gauzy fabric with several purposes, including scenery and lighting.

Segue: used in musicals to refer to the act or scene that immediately follows another.

Show cloth: a piece of material that contains the logo or title of a specific show; usually travels with a company for easy display in each venue.

Show report: report provided by stage management detailing any problems from the previous performance; actors and technical staff receive copies so that problems can be addressed.

Sightlines: lines that are drawn on plans and diagrams to identify the areas of the stage that are visible to the extreme seating areas of the audience.

Silk: light filter used to stretch light in a particular direction.

Snap: refers to a cue that has no fade time; usually a lighting or sound cue.

Soliloquy: refers to an oration by an actor on stage when they are speaking to themselves.

Spike: occurs when someone marks the position of a prop or a piece of the set on stage.

Stage door keeper: a member of the theatrical crew, positioned inside the stage door whose role is to know each actor and member of the technical staff, know fire safety procedures for the theatre, greet visitors and press, and pass messages between any parties.

Stagger-through: the first run-through of a performance.

Stalls: refers to the audience's seating that is just below stage level.

Stock scenery: pieces of scenery that are kept in storage to be used throughout several performances.

Strike: the disassembling of stage sets.

TBC: acronym that stands for to be confirmed; usually seen in a cast list

when an actor has not been chosen for a part or if a venue or date has not yet been selected.

Throw: refers to the distance between a light source and the person or item being lit.

Thrust: refers to a stage that reaches forward into the auditorium and has audience seating on at least two sides; also called a *theatre in the round*.

Thunder run: a channel down which a cannonball can be run to simulate the sound of thunder.

Thunder sheet: sheet of metal that can be shaken using two attached handles, or beaten, to simulate the sound of thunder.

Tilt: refers to the up-and-down movement of a lantern.

Tormentors: screens or curtains that are usually set up at right angles to the proscenium arch to keep the audience from seeing activity occurring off-stage.

Transformation: refers to an immediate scene change that involves the use of gauze and lighting to hide or show certain areas of the stage.

Trap: an opening built into the stage floor.

Grave trap: a rectangular drop-down, resembling a grave, built into a stage floor.

Cauldron trap: a trap built into a stage floor to facilitate placing items into a prop (such as a cauldron) from beneath the stage.

Star trap: refers to a trap that has multiple triangular hinged doors through which an actor can enter the stage from below.

Trap room: the room directly under the trap door of a stage.

Traverse-: theatre set-up in which the audience is seated on either side of the acting area.

Treads: refers to stairs or steps connected to a stage area.

Typecast: term used to refer to an actor who is repeatedly cast in a similar role.

Upper circle: usually raked seating in a theatre, located at the highest level in the auditorium.

Upstage: refers to the part of the acting stage that is farthest away from the audience seating; may also be used to refer to the undesirable movement of one actor while on stage that causes another actor to turn their back towards the audience.

Ushers: theatre staff members who lead audience to their seats; ushers are often seated in the auditorium during performances in case of an emergency.

Visual cue: a cue based on the action on stage rather than given by a stage manager.

Vomitory: entrance to the auditorium located in the banked seating areas.

Wagon stage: complex scenery device in which bulky set items are positioned on sliding trucks, the width of the proscenium arch, mechanized to allow for quick scene changes.

Walk-on: acting role that requires the actor be physically present on stage but not speak.

Wash: a lighting cover that blankets the whole stage in a certain type or color of light.

Wings: the sides of the stage that are not in the audience's line of sight; may also refer to scenery that is set up at the point where the acting area meets the technical area.

Wipe: refers to a single curtain that slides across a stage to hide it from view; may also be used as a backdrop or a part of the scenery.

Yo-yo: the device used by lighting technicians to remotely adjust a *gobo* while it is set in a lantern.

Tab track: the track that holds a moveable horizontal curtain that can be used to hide the stage or used as a backdrop for scenery.

Tabs: curtains that are horizontally suspended to hide the stage area or are used as part of a backdrop.

An **A-D converter** is an analog-to-digital converter, used in computer soundcards. It converts a varying electrical signal into binary data.

ALD stands for "Association of Lighting Designers."

A1-code is the code used by the Lighting Industry Forum to identify the recommended usage of various lamps. A1 lamps are recommended for projection.

Absorption is a surface's ability to absorb sound.

Acoustics refers to the behavior of sound in certain areas and usually depends upon the size and shape of a space, as well as the presence of any sound-absorbing materials.

The **acting area** is the space on a stage or in another performance space in which an actor can move while remaining in full view of the audience.

The **acting edition** refers to the script that contains notes for actors or technicians and may be written by the playwright or the premiere production staff.

Ad lib occurs when an actor must improvise lines or actions to compensate for forgetting their own or for another actor's lapse in memory.

An **advance bar** is a lighting bar that is set up downstage of the proscenium arch.

An **aero** is a light with a tight beam that produces very intense light, originally used as an aircraft landing light.

Ambient noise is the sound that exists in a room when no sound sources are present.

Ampere, called "amps" are the units of measurement that refer to the electrical current passing through a circuit.

An **Amplifier** is a piece of sound equipment that converts a low voltage signal into a higher current signal.

Lighting

Lighting in theatre can be used in several ways. The most basic purpose of theatre lighting is to allow the audience to see what is happening on stage. Lighting is also useful for providing depth to the stage and actors. The use of highlights and shadows, called *modeling*, creates a three-dimensional effect. Lighting can serve an overall compositional purpose by helping to create a series of connected imagery that brings the director's interpretation to life. It can be used to give information about the setting of a play, pinpointing the time of day, the season and location. Light can also be used to focus the audience's attention on a particular element of the production or to create a mood for a play. The proper lighting can reflect the emotional content of a performance lending to a cohesive and balanced production.

Elements controlled by lighting designers
Light has six primary qualities that can be controlled by lighting designers: intensity, color, direction, distribution, texture and movement. *Intensity* is the light that is reflected by a performer and the background. It can be controlled by use of dimmers, colored gels and the type of light source used. *Color* is the color of the light reflected by the actor and background. It can be controlled through use of colored gels, lamp temperatures and dimmers. *Direction*, the angle of the light, determines the size and direction of shadows. *Light placement* is crucial in controlling direction and *distribution* refers to the part of the stage that will receive lighting. Distribution is controlled by the type of lighting, the focus of the light, masking devices and the direction of the light source. *Texture* refers to the degree of diffusion or clarity in a light source. Texture is determined by the type of light, diffusion gels and screening devices. Intensity and color can be greatly affected by costumes, makeup and props. *Movement* refers to changes in intensity, direction, distribution, color and texture.

Properties of light
The properties of stage lighting include intensity, color, direction, distribution, texture and movement. Each function of stage lighting can be achieved in various ways through the manipulation of the properties of light. Visibility can be altered by the use of intensity, color and direction. Intensity and distribution determine the focus of stage lighting. Modeling is primarily achieved through the manipulation of light direction. Information, like visibility, can be achieved by the use of intensity, color and direction. For example, daytime scenes have brighter lighting than nighttime scenes. The mood of a play can be altered through use of the light properties of intensity, color, direction and distribution. The overall mood of a comedy is often best projected in warm, bright light while tragedies have darker lighting. The manipulation of all these functions and properties determines the success of the composite function of lighting, which serves to create a coherent production.

Types of lights
The profile spot, also called the ellipsoidal reflector spotlight, provides a hard-edged beam of light. Profile spots offer a beam that has a fixed size with a high intensity and very little stray light. Templates or stencils called *gobos* can be inserted into profile spots to cast a specific image or affect. The Fresnel spot offers a soft-edged beam with controllable size. Soft-edged lights like the Fresnel spot are used to light adjacent stage areas because the soft edges allow the lighting to overlap without creating any hard edges. The pebble-convex offers a semi-hard-edged

beam. Like profile spots, pebble-convex lights have little or no stray light. The par is used when an intense and fixed beam of light is needed. Pars can be compared to the headlights of a car. The floodlight is used to flood a large area with light.

Profile spotlight: The profile spot works by reflecting a lamp's light and then passing the light through a gate. A plano-convex lens is used to focus the light and the gate has four shutters that can be moved in order to shape the light beam. Gate runners are built into the light to allow for irises and gobos to be inserted. Irises are devices that control the circular size of the light beam. Gobos are stencils that create patterns of light and shadow. For example, a gobo could be inserted to cast the image of a windowpane. The intensity of the light depends on the size of the beam, with narrow beams producing the highest intensity. The light can be *flat-field* or *peak*. Flat-field means that the light is evenly distributed throughout the beam. Peak refers to the higher concentration of light at the center of the beam. Profiles often have two lenses, one of which can be adjusted to control the size of the beam, while the other is adjusted to control the focus.

Floodlights: Floodlights are used to flood an area with light. There are three types of floodlights: *evenly spread*, *bottom concentration* and *battens*. Evenly spread floodlights provide light to a large area with every part of the beam emitting the same amount of light. Floodlights that are concentrated on the bottom emit a heavier light in the lower part of the beam, achieved by shaping the reflector part of the floodlight with an epitaxial lamp. Battens are created when floodlights are attached in long strips and used to light specific areas. Battens that are set up on the stage floor are called ground rows, those used on the front edge of the stage are called footlights and

battens suspended from the ceiling are called border lights or magazine battens.

Terms relating to stage lighting
- The lighting structure, which can include side lights, top lights and back lights, refers to the manner in which lights are set up to fall upon the stage and the actors.
- Flat front light is a lighting technique in which a beam is focused directly on an actor's face. Flat front light is often used to correct for key lighting, which can decrease the visibility of an actor's eyes. Using flat front light can correct this by making the actor's eyes more visible. Flat lighting can also be cast at a 45-degree angle for a more flattering look.
- Key light refers to the main source of lighting in a particular scene. Key lighting often creates unintentional areas of shadow, which are lit by fill lights.
- Side lighting involves lights that are set up on the sides of the stage above the actors' heads, allowing the actors to be seen when they are facing the sides of the stage.
- Backlight, top light and bottom light are all basic lighting structures. Backlights, positioned to shine down upon an actor or scene from above and behind the subject, are used to separate the actor from the background as they create an intense halo around the head and shoulders of the actor. Backlighting does not alter the faces of the actors, so various colored backlights can easily be used to create a mood on the stage.
- Top lights, also called downlights, are positioned directly above the subject, shining on protruding facial and body features, which provides a high contrast.

- Bottom light is also called uplight. Uplights are positioned in front of and beneath the subject. This is a rare technique because it is a very unnatural lighting angle. Footlights are considered types of uplights. Uplights can provide a very eerie effect, which you can picture by imagining what happens when someone shines a flashlight up from their chin, a common technique used while telling ghost stories around a campfire.

Sound technicians' tools

In the early days of theatre, sound was created by any means available. For example, the sound of thunder was simulated by rolling a cannonball down a narrow trench carved into the roof of a theatre. Now the sound of thunder can be created through use of digital sound equipment. Technicians have the ability to reproduce sounds made by things like doorbells and telephones. Technicians can also reinforce these sounds through use of amplification. The variety of technology available now allows for technicians to reproduce nearly any sound needed for a performance. Background music and actors' voices can all be controlled through use of speakers, microphones and soundboards. Sound quality is a crucial part of any theatre experience and a successful performance allows the audience to both see and hear the performance without distraction.

Costume designing

The costume designer's role is very important in helping to achieve the director's vision. The costumes should contribute to the tone and style of a production and the time period in which the play is set must be taken into account. It is important to consider the many facets of a character's personality and lifestyle, including their job and social status. The costumes also serve to differentiate or unify certain characters. For example, a play in which the characters are divided between servants and the aristocracy should involve two distinct costuming groups. Costumes must also be practical for the actors, allowing them to move freely and change quickly. It is important for costume designers to consult with the director in order to ensure that the costume designs will be consistent with the theme of the production.

Editing and video installation

Montage, or editing, is probably the one discipline unique to film, video, and television. The timing, rhythm and progression of shots forms the ultimate composition of the film. This procedure is one of the most critical elements of post-production and incorporates sound editing and mixing, as well as the design and execution of digital special effects.

In the case of a video installation, the method of presentation becomes critical. The work may be screened on a simple monitor, projected on a wall or other surface or incorporated into a larger sculptural installation. A video installation may also involve sound, with similar considerations to be made based on speaker design and placement, volume and tone.

Drama

Classicism
Classicism is a theatrical style developed by French playwrights in the 17th century. In general, classicism places emphasis on society, reason and enlightenment. Classicism as a theatrical style incorporates the rules and traditions of

ancient Greek and Roman theatre, embodying Aristotle's theories regarding the unity of time, place and action.

Neo-classicism

Neoclassicism is a product of the 18th century. Neoclassicism, as a theatrical style, is characterized by extravagant costumes and elaborate scenery with stories that involve a high degree of melodrama. Neoclassic theatre has clearly defined genres of either tragedy or comedy.

Elizabethan

Elizabethan theatre is characterized by a high number of characters, several subplots that eventually merge and a varied mixture of emotion.

Restoration

Restoration drama, also known as the comedy of manners, is characterized by witty dialogue with themes of virtue and honor. Restoration theatre also featured plots involving the sexual behavior of sophisticated society. ~~20090427.41495.250~~

Romanticism

Romanticism was the dominant style from 1750 to 1800. Romanticism is characterized by mankind's unfaltering trust in the kindness of nature. Reason was regarded as secondary to instinct and logic was forsaken for emotion. Romantic ideals encouraged the idea that a simple life was the most desirable kind. Romanticism allowed for the glorification of past civilizations, especially that of the Greeks. It also boasted the merit of the natural man in a primitive setting such as Native Americans. Romantic ideals encouraged the elimination of social classes and the heightened sense of detail. Romanticism fused comic and tragic styles into a unified form of drama that favored the individual actor above the type actor. Romanticism also favored abstraction and idealism. Romantic

dramas had a tendency to use special effects because the style focused on visual appeal.

Realism

The ideology of realism was based on science and technology, suggesting that science could solve the problems of humanity. Realism stressed that truth was that which could be felt by the five senses and was characterized by contemporary settings and periods. The themes of realist drama were common to everyday people.

Naturalism

Naturalism, a branch of realism, was developed as a result of the work of Charles Darwin. Darwin's theories on evolution materialized into a form of drama with a prevailing pessimistic attitude in which there was no climax.

Expressionist

The goal of expressionist theatre was to express raw emotion, not to teach, entertain or duplicate reality. Expressionism is characterized by highly exaggerated movements and voice techniques to express the emotion of the characters. Expressionism also tends to dramatize the struggles and spiritual nature of protagonists as well as the struggles between differing social classes.

Absurdist

Absurdist drama is characterized by a lack of realistic characters, an ambiguous concept of time and a vague attempt to define the setting.

Types of plays

Chronicle plays

Chronicle plays are historical dramas based on English history written primarily during the Elizabethan and Jacobean periods. The source of many of these plays was Holinshed's "Chronicles of England, Scotland, and Ireland", thus the title "Chronicle Plays".

Mystery plays

Mystery Plays are dramatic works based on the Bible. These dramas were usually produced by local trade guilds for the pleasure of their villages. They were presented in cycles that sometimes dramatized the entire New and Old Testaments. Mystery plays were performed in England, France, Spain, and Italy, among other countries. Passion plays are specialized mystery plays based on the passion of Christ.

Heroic dramas

Heroic Dramas featured heroes of epic deeds. Usually written in blank verse or heroic couplets, these plays reached the apex of their popularity during the Restoration period.

Interludes

Interlude refers to a very short form of drama sometimes performed between courses of a banquet but also the term came to refer to any kind of musical or dramatic entertainment. These were usually performed for private parties and fell out of favor with the opening of public venues. Their popularity peaked in 16th century England.

Nos

No is a form of traditional Japanese theatre that use music, dance, and poetry. They make no claim to be realistic, rather creating a serene and peaceful mood through spectacle and imagery. No are based on eastern religions, reflecting themes from Hinduism and Buddhism. The plays have a fixed repertory that has been constant since the 1500's. William Butler Yeats adapted No for western audiences in a series of short plays. They remain popular with drama critics and certain classes of Japanese.

Problem plays

Problem plays focus on social problems and movements. Alexander Dumas, son of the great French novelist, wrote a series of short plays attacking the ills of society. The early 19th century was the heyday of problem plays. Henrik Ibsen is perhaps the most celebrated playwright of problem plays, particularly with his treatment of women's rights in "The Doll House". Lillian Hellman and Arthur Miller have both written popular problem plays in the 20th century.

The term "problem plays" is used in a different context by Shakespearean scholars. These critics use the term for plays that have caused interpretation problems for audiences. Plays such as "All's Well That Ends Well", "Troilus and Cressida", and "Measure for Measure" lend themselves to various interpretations and pose literary problems for students of the bard.

Farce

A farce is a dramatic comedy that is full of action, escapades of characters always on the brink of disaster, and full of stereotypical characters filling stock roles. The farce is one of the oldest forms of comedy, found in folk plays, Greek drama, the Renaissance and modern theatre. The 'Bedroom farce' is a special type of comedy based on the foibles of attempted seductions. It continues to be popular in modern theatre, notably in the work of Alan Ayckbourn. The theater of the absurd uses farce to represent the essential meaninglessness and chaos of life. Specialized forms of this are tragic farce, which combines farce with tragedy. Farce is perhaps best known by the public through silent films, where Charlie Chaplin, the Keystone Cops and many other slapstick comedians made film an excellent example of farce enjoyed by a wide audience.

Aristotle's six elements of drama

Aristotle identified six elements that define drama: spectacle, sound, diction, character, idea and action. These six elements are, according to Aristotle, what every drama has in common. Modern critics combine the elements of action, character and idea into the single element of plot.

- *Action* is any physical, mental or emotional activity performed by a character.
- The term *character* refers to the physical, mental or emotional qualities demonstrated by actors allowing the audience to see them as unique individuals.
- *Idea* is defined as the theme that the author is attempting to convey to the audience. These three elements can comprise plot; however, it is possible for any one of these elements to be dominant.
- *Diction* refers to the language of the play. The language is a crucial element, as it reveals both overt and subtle information about characters and situations in a play.
- *Music* refers to the actual music used in a play as well as all other auditory devices, which can include the rhythm of spoken lines and sound effects.
- *Spectacle* refers to the visual elements of a play. These include make-up, costumes and sets.

Action

Aristotle defined six elements of drama: spectacle, sound, diction, character, idea and action. Modern critics have elaborated upon these elements. Aristotle's original element of action is comprised of eight sub-elements: exposition, problem, point of attack, foreshadowing, complications, crises, climax, and denouement. *Exposition* provides the audience with information about the time period, setting, characters,

relationships and events of the play. The *problem* is the event that sets the plot in motion. The *point of attack* is the way the author presents the problem. The author may have the problem occur before or after the main character is introduced. *Foreshadowing* refers to the clues planted by the writer that will result in a believable finish. *Complication* is the event that occurs after the problem is introduced. The complication is the obstacle that could prevent the character from achieving a goal. The *crisis* is the point where the character must make a crucial decision or undergo a significant event. The height of the crisis is the *climax*, which represents the peak of the entire plot. The story finally concludes with the *denouement*.

Key aspects of drama

Theme
Ideas or concepts given sustained attention in a drama highlight the major themes of the work. Often the title of the play reflects themes to be presented.

Argument
Some works are really expositions of arguments and points that the author wants to make. Arguments and themes are given dramatic force through the form in which they are expressed. This could be action, speech, or narration.

Patterns of imagery
These include the use of symbols and keywords. These are recurring motifs that form themes and plot development together. Some plays focus on a particular image. Symbols are subtle devices used by authors for a variety of reasons, and they are usually a key to the major themes of the drama. Symbols may change as the play progresses, and these changes are important in plotting and action. Some key words are used as symbols, and are repeated and emphasized to enrich the material. These

keywords may be tied to one character or shared by many.

Progression of a dramatic plot

When studying dramatic works, significant events in the story should be recognized. Major shifts or reversals in the plot, and subsequent action should be followed carefully. Aristotle's "Poetics" described a typical progression pattern of a plot as follows:
- Exposition
- Complication
- Reversal
- Recognition
- Resolution

This progression is still valid today as we study and analyze plots. The plot may follow the pattern of comedy (ending with a celebration), or tragedy (ending with death). The plot may be explained through dialogue, stage action, and off-stage events or by a chorus. While plots of well known plays are easily understood and analyzed, more esoteric drama requires more careful attention to the plot's complexities.

Advancing the plot

Authors use many devices to maintain interest and advance the plot. Among these are building tension between characters, creating difficult situations that cannot easily be resolved, and highlighting conflict and romance. Often authors choose not to reveal some information that increases tension. Action is the physical events in a play. Action can be important or have little dramatic impact. Some plays depend on spectacles rather than dialogue to emphasize plot and characters. Staging is an important element in the action of a drama. The play may be written for a particular acting space, necessary for the action employed. The theatre the play was written to be performed in often dictates the scope of action in the work. A work requiring lavish spectacles is usually not written for small theatres. Adaptations may be made in specific productions to allow more or less" action space".

Knowledge of characters

In order to understand a dramatic work, detailed knowledge of major characters is essential. Details of their past, motivations for their actions, fatal flaws, romantic relationships, antagonistic characters, and historical context all weave a tapestry of characters that fill out a drama's skeleton. It is vital to distinguish between major characters, who are central to the drama and minor ones who are only functional. The extent to which each character is developed is a good clue in identifying major and minor personae. Details of the relationships between characters often are an excellent guide to plot development and resolution. Who loves whom, who hates whom, who are allied, who are enemies, and the implications of these tangled webs form the structure of plot and drama. Of the many possible relationships in a play, only a few will be crucial. These should be identified and followed closely.

Speech and dialogue

Analysis of speech and dialogue is important in the critical study of drama. Some playwrights use speech to develop their characters. Speeches may be long or short, and written in as normal prose or blank verse. Some characters have a unique way of speaking which illuminates aspects of the drama. Emphasis and tone are both important, as well. Does the author make clear the tone in which lines are to be spoken, or is this open to interpretation? Sometimes there are various possibilities in tone with regard to delivering lines.

Asides and soliloquies

Asides and soliloquies can be important in plot and character development. Asides indicate that not all characters are privy to the lines. This may be a method of advancing or explaining the plot in a subtle manner. Soliloquies are opportunities for character development, plot enhancement, and to give insight to characters motives, feelings, and emotions. Careful study of these elements provides a reader with an abundance of clues to the major themes and plot of the work.

Apostrophe and soliloquy

Apostrophe occurs when a character addresses an abstract idea or a persona not present in the scene. This differs from a soliloquy where a character seems to be speaking to himself, or thinking out loud. The soliloquy was used extensively in English Renaissance drama and made popular by Shakespeare in his dramatic works. The soliloquy has evolved into interior monologues in fiction where the musings of a character are used to develop depth and advance plots. Apostrophe and soliloquy are often confused, and it should be remembered that a soliloquy occurs when there is only one character on the stage, while in apostrophe there may be other characters in the scene but not addressed.

Antistrophe

Antistrophe is a device in Greek drama where the chorus responds to a previous stanza of verse. Antistrophe is rarely seen today outside of the production of classical Greek drama.

Agony

Agony is the Greek word for struggle or conflict. As used in classical Greek drama, it indicates a portion of the play in which two characters engage in a heated argument or debate. Each of the characters is supported in their arguments by a part of the Greek chorus. The agony is a device used extensively in both comedies and tragedies. It is often the part of Greek drama when climaxes of the plot unfold. The opposing characters usually represent conflicting themes or ideas in the drama. In tragedies the agony is sometimes followed by the death or exile of the protagonist.

In modern literature the term is used in literary criticism to denote a competitive battle. Harold Bloom used the term as an element in literary history in terms of the conflict between a major poet and his or her predecessor whom the poet feels he must displace.

Chorus

Utilized in Greek drama, the chorus is a group of actors who furnish a commentary on the play as it unfolds. The chorus in Greek drama probably evolved from the choral tradition of musical productions. Traditionally, the chorus speaks for society rather than any character in the play. This means the chorus is the objective observer of the dramatic action. Shakespeare occasionally used the chorus in some of his plays. Henry V and Romeo and Juliet are examples of this. In musical dramas, the term refers to a group of singers and dancers who play an important part of the production. Modern drama usually does not employ a chorus, although it was used in T.S. Eliot's play "Murder in the Cathedral" in 1935. The chorus in modern musical theatre often acts a collective actor that adds to the spectacle of the production.

Sociolinguistics

Copyright © Mometrix Media. You have been licensed one copy of this document for personal use only. Any other reproduction or redistribution is strictly prohibited. All rights reserved.

Sociolinguistics is the study of the relationship between language and the structure of society. It takes into account the social backgrounds of both the speaker and the addressee, the relationship between the speaker and the addressee, and the context and manner of the interaction. Because the emphasis in sociolinguistics is on language use, the analysis of language in this field is typically based on taped recordings of everyday interactions. The sociolinguists seek to discover universal properties of languages, attempting to analyze questions such as "do all languages change in the same ways"? Answers are sought to the larger questions about universals in society in which language plays a major role. The multifaceted nature of language and its broad impact on many areas of society make this field an exciting and cutting edge part of linguistics.

Aesthetics

Aesthetics is the study of sensory or sensori-emotional values, sometimes called judgments of sentiment and taste. Aesthetics is a subdiscipline of axiology, a branch of philosophy, and is closely associated with the philosophy of art. Aesthetics studies new ways of seeing and of perceiving the world. Judgments of aesthetic value clearly rely on our ability to discriminate at a sensory level. Aesthetics examines what makes something beautiful, sublime, disgusting, fun, cute, silly, entertaining, pretentious, discordant, harmonious, boring, humorous or tragic.

Aesthetic judgments usually go beyond sensory discrimination. For David Hume, delicacy of taste is not merely "the ability to detect all the ingredients in a composition," but also our sensitivity "to pains as well as pleasures, which escape the rest of mankind." Thus, the sensory discrimination is linked to a capacity for pleasure. For Immanuel Kant, "enjoyment" is the result when pleasure arises from sensation, but judging something to be "beautiful" has a third requirement: sensation must give rise to pleasure by engaging our capacities of reflective contemplation. Judgments of beauty are sensory, emotional, and intellectual all at once.

Aesthetics in film

Film combines many diverse disciplines, each of which may have its own rules of aesthetics. The aesthetics of cinematography are closely related to still photography, but the movement of the subject(s) or the camera and the intensities, colors, and placement of the lighting are highly important. Sound recording, editing, and mixing are other highly important areas of film, often closely related to the musical score. As in theatre, art direction in the design of the sets and shooting locations also applies, as does costume design and makeup. All of these disciplines are closely intertwined and must be brought together by the aesthetic sensibilities of the director.

Performing arts and aesthetics

Performing arts appeal to our aesthetics of storytelling, grace, balance, class, timing, strength, shock, humor, costume, irony, beauty, drama, suspense and sensuality. Whereas live stage performance is usually constrained by the physical reality at hand, film performance can further add the aesthetic elements of large-scale action, fantasy, and a complex interwoven musical score. Performance art often consciously mixes the aesthetics of several forms. Role-playing games are sometimes seen as a performing art with an aesthetic structure of their own, called *RPG theory*.

Aesthetic judgment

Aesthetic judgment is a philosophy that questions the legitimacy of people's

- 40 -

notions of what is pleasing to their tastes. Early puritanical thought equated beauty with pleasure, and pleasure was seen as evil. As the idea of aesthetic judgment evolved, it became the consensus that one should not like something because it was pleasurable to their senses but that like of something should be supported by one's ability to reconcile that object with the tools of their education and knowledge. Philosopher Immanuel Kant proposed that beauty should be judged both for its subjectivity and universality. Scottish philosopher David Hume also published a series of works on the validity of aesthetic judgment. In his essay on the aesthetic of tragedy, he explained that tragedy could be a pleasurable experience because even though it provokes a sense of sadness, it also produces a sense of delight in the viewing of a theatrical production. In such cases, Hume claims, the conflicting emotions of pleasure and displeasure are balanced by each other and balanced emotion results in pleasure.

Egyptian passion plays

One of the earliest preserved documents attesting to the existence of dramatic productions is a stone tablet from 2000 B.C. The tablet contains a description of the roles played by the Egyptian king Ikhernofret. The ancient productions are believed to resemble today's passion plays and served as a means to communicate the suffering and successes of a particular deity. Like modern passion plays, the ancient forms showed the trials faced by the god and ended with the resurrection of the god. Egyptian passion plays generally centered around the central god figure of Osiris, whose legend claims that he was murdered by his brother, but later resurrected. Osiris is often seen as the god who rules over the underworld. Records indicate that passion plays depicting the life of Osiris occurred annually in the cities of Abydos and Heliopolis.

Origin of comedy

According to Aristotle, comedy was first introduced in a performance or festival called *komos*. Komos was an ancient Greek ritual in which a group of drunken males danced and sang, often in a procession, while carrying a large phallus. The phallic symbol was a tribute to the god Phales, believed to be the companion of Bacchus, the god of wine. Greek celebrations often ended with a group of young males parading in the city streets with torches in hand. Members of the group, called *comoedus*, were led in song by a flute- or lyre-player. The activity was known as a *comus* or *komos*. Aristotle further claimed that these events could be traced back to the Greek cities of Megaris and Sicyon. Aristotle supported this theory on the origins of comedy by stating that the first comic poet, Susarion, was an inhabitant of a town very near Megaris.

Origin of tragedy

According to Aristotle, tragedy can be traced to the Greek songs called *dithyrambs*, which were sung in honor of the fertility god Dionysus. Greek men would dance while wearing costumes of goatskins in order to impersonate satyrs, as these were the constant companions of Dionysus. The song sung by these men was called a *tragoedia*, which means "goat-song" in Greek. This ritual was expanded upon by the addition of a central male figure to which the songs were addressed. The central male figure would answer questions sung to him by the surrounding circle males or chorus. The word *chorus* is derived from the Greek word "choros," which meant to dance in a circle. There are many differing views on the exact origin of the tragedy, but the above describes the basic consensus among scholars.

William Ridgeway's theory:

In 1904, the interpretation of Aristotle's origins of tragedy came into question. Scholars began to question Aristotle's theory as well as modern man's interpretation of this theory. William Ridgeway, a writer and scholar, published a book in which he presented the theory that tragedy originated not from the worship of the god Dionysus but from the worship of the dead. This completely changed the geographical origins of Aristotle's theory because the worship of the dead was much more widespread. Ridgeway believed that the cult of Dionysus was introduced to the city of Sicyon by the statesman Cleisthenes. Ridgeway further explained that Dionysus was worshipped as a hero among the Greeks because he was a mortal man who became a saint and was elevated to god-like status. Ridgeway supported his theory by offering as evidence the fact that Dionysus, like most dead kings of the time, had an oracle within his temple. Based on this knowledge, the worship of Dionysus is actually the worship of the dead, making both Aristotle and Ridgeway's theories correct.

Elements of tragedy

A tragedy is a play in which a heroic character, through unfortunate circumstances, experiences a downfall. The unfortunate circumstances are usually orchestrated by the gods as a punishment for the sin of *hubris*, the sin of pride. It is common for the hero to have a desire to attain some type of power that would liken them to a god. The constraints of mortality would not allow a human to achieve a goal or attain a power that is reserved for gods. The hero in a tragedy is usually depicted as a likeable but flawed character who begins the tragedy as an ignorant being but ends the tragedy as an enlightened being. The events that unfold are such that they change the hero's life and manner of thinking. The hero is not required to die

to learn his lesson, but must go through a major change or enlightenment as the tragedy progresses.

Characteristics of Greek comedy

Old Greek comedy

The year of 450 B.C. marks the approximate start of *Old Comedy*, which evolved from the celebrations of the god Dionysus. Old Comedy was best known for its crude language and lack of restriction. Dramatists of Old Comedy were allowed to exercise poetic license to its fullest extent. It was common for the actors to verbally attack, ridicule and defame a well-known person who was generally disliked by the populace of Greece. Old Comedy served both as a source of entertainment and as a front for political campaigns. In order to best understand plays written in the time of Old Comedy, modern readers should take time to study the political climate of the time period in which the work was written. Although Old Comedy differed from Greek tragedies, the two also shared some attributes, such as the vital role of the chorus. Unlike the tragic plays of that time, Old Comedy did not use myths and legends as a basis for plot.

Middle Greek comedy

Middle Comedy was the dominant form of Greek comedy from the end of the fifth century to the middle of the fourth century B.C. Middle Comedy differed from its predecessor in that it lacked the chorus. This was the first time the importance of the chorus was diminished in theatre. Prior to Middle Comedy, Old Comedy and tragedy had emphasized the role of the chorus. Unlike Old Comedy, Middle Comedy ceased to impersonate public characters on stage, diminishing the use of theatre as a political outlet. The focus of Middle Comedy shifted to fictional characters rather than current or historical figures. Middle Comedy introduced the comic figure of the sharp-tongued cook, present in many Greek plays.

New Greek comedy

New Comedy was the genre that ruled the Greek stage from the late fourth century through 260 B.C. New Comedy was largely focused on the idea of unrequited or unattainable love and introduced the character of the mercenary soldier returning home from war. This form had no characters likened to public figures or heroes. Rather, the characters of New Comedy were common people who faced everyday problems. This new genre completely eliminated the chorus and was received well by audiences because the nature of its plays involved universal themes. The use of these common themes allowed for New Comedy to translate well in other geographic regions and it subsequently spread to Rome, Italy and to England. This ancient form of New Comedy was the foundation for the comic forms used in theatre and television today.

Ancient Athenian drama

Athenian drama was seen as not only a source of entertainment but also as a religious celebration. The religious connection was a result of the fact that Athenian plays were performed only twice a year, usually during the two Dionysian festivals. Since the entertainment of the masses was considered a governmental duty, theatrical productions of ancient Athens were managed by the state. The state chose playwrights and actors while the wealthy upper-class citizens footed the bill. Plays were performed from morning to night during several days of the festivals. Generally, the performances were contests in which the winning poet was given a prize by the state. Almost every Athenian citizen would attend these productions and the twenty-thousand plus capacity of the theatre ensured that

everyone could attend. The poets and playwrights chosen by the state received the great privilege of being heard by the entirety of Athens and it for this reason that these ancient artists had such a great impact on the manner in which we now view those times.

Origins of satire

While most ancient forms of theatre are credited to the Greeks, satire was the invention of the Romans. The Roman satire was a tool used to criticize the current social situation. Roman satire took one of two forms: *Menippean* or *verse*. Menippean satire was named for its originator, Greek cynic Mennipus and is characterized by a rhapsodic blending of prose and verse that ridiculed various social characters. Seneca's work entitled *The Apocolocyntosis* is an example of the Menippean satire. Verse satire, created by Lucilius but most readily seen in the works of Horace, was generally composed in epic meter. The Roman satire bore a similarity to the Greek form of Old Comedy in that both were a means of attacking the injustices perpetuated by the political climate of the time.

Satyr plays of the early Greeks

Pratinus is recognized as the first writer of the Greek *satyr play*. Satyrs were the half-man, half-goat companions of the god Dionysus. In the early Greek plays, a group of males wearing goat costumes danced and sang in an act of worship directed towards the god Dionysus. These groups of goat-skinned dancers were impersonating satyrs and evolved into what became known as the *chorus* in many Greek tragedies. The chorus of satyrs, generally prone to merriment, were not appropriate accompaniment for the more serious Greek tragedies, so their role was increasingly diminished over time. In order to preserve the fun-natured spirit of the satyr chorus, Pratinus began to compose short plays in which this group took center stage. Athenian theatre became organized into *tetralogies*, compilations of three tragedies followed by one satiric piece. The purpose of including the satyr form was to allow the audience to recover from the serious nature of the tragedy by enjoying the more light-hearted jests of the satyr chorus.

Preservation of Greek plays

It was the responsibility of the Athenian archons, or magistrates, to maintain records of Greek productions. They recorded names of the upper-class citizens who financed the productions, the poets, actors, plays and contest winners. These records were later published by Aristotle. Athenians had an insatiable appetite for theatre, as their normal viewings were limited to only a few days of the year. In order to satisfy the need for theatre during the off-season, many of the great plays of that time were rewritten by people known as *adapters*. To preserve the integrity of the original work, the law required that the distribution of any copy of an original work had to be recorded by a public secretary. The library at Alexandria holds copies of various tragic and satyr plays. The most common of the ancient Greek plays seen today are those that were preserved for use in educational institutions of the Middle Ages, including the works of Aeschylus, Sophocles, Euripides and Aristophanes.

Origins of Roman theatre

Roman theatre can easily be traced to Greek roots, as the Romans borrowed much of their theatre from Greek poets, even using Greek actors in Roman productions. It is believed that Rome had no intrinsic growth of poetry; rather, it was transplanted into Roman culture during a time when the Roman population sought to cultivate exotic luxuries. Livius Andronicus is credited with being the first Roman to imitate the theatre of the Greeks and is therefore credited with bringing theatre to Rome. The forms that were most easily converted from Greek to Roman were that of *New Comedy* and *tragedy*. Prior to Andronicus, the earliest spoken Roman productions were those of the Italian-import known as the *Atellan Fables*. The Greek form of theatre, in its transfer to Roman culture, was altered to better suit its Roman audience. The chorus, which historically sat in the orchestra area of the theatre, was removed, leaving the orchestra occupied by high-ranking spectators. Comedies were more easily received in Roman theatre than were tragedies.

Experience of attending a Roman play
Roman theatre usually consisted of a daytime production that lasted for approximately two hours, plays being most often performed immediately before or after the noon meal. Comedy was the dominant form of Roman theatre, using masks, wigs, costumes and makeup. Women were forbidden from participation in these plays, leaving the role of any female characters to be played by young boys. The earliest Roman venues consisted of very basic amphitheatres where the audience reclined on the ground and actors had very few resources at their disposal. As theatre evolved, the Roman stage was composed of a common street with several houses in the background and

audiences were entertained by flute players during scene changes. Pompey the Great built the first Roman theatre auditorium in the year 55 B.C., where audiences were most entertained by outrageous and crude spectacles.

Roman tragedy

Romans favored comedy above tragedy as a form of theatre, thus few tragic works have been preserved. The writings of Seneca provide the most notable remnants of the Roman tragedy. Additionally, Marcus Pacuvius and Lucius Accius are both noted for their imitations of Greek tragedy. The failure of the evolution of tragedy as a theatrical form in the hands of the Romans is in part due to their inability to reconcile the elements of song, dance and dialogue. The Romans seemed only able to successfully produce either a song and dance *or* a dialogue. The song and dance form evolved into a comedy that later lent itself to the *pantomimus*, or modern day mime. Dialogue was used to enact tragic productions, usually involving one actor reciting tales to a small audience.

Decline of Roman drama

The Roman theatre offered little entertainment for citizens, as their daily lives were already filled with shocking drama. It was common for Romans to see crucifixions, chained slaves paraded through streets and men killed by beasts in arena shows. The Roman culture had little tolerance socially or politically for the offerings of the theatre. They were more concerned with the matters of law than with the matters of the heart. The theatre productions borrowed from the Greeks were of a light-hearted and witty nature, lost on the Roman population, most of whom were unable to comprehend what they considered such trifles. The Roman Empire continued its expansion, requiring that the ruling class be distributed among newly acquired territories, which led to an overall decrease in the number of upper-class citizens in Rome. The remaining citizens, who were undereducated, were unable to understand the classical Latin language that was common in the theatre and were more intrigued by arena shows and circus performers than theatrics. The religious conversion of Roman emperor Constantine led to the outlaw of drama by Christian churches.

Dramatic literature in the Middle Ages

With the spread of Christianity, drama was outlawed as a vile and blasphemous spectacle. Rome experienced a fall from grace as the city of Constantinople became the new capital of civilization, during which time drama was mostly extinct. However, theatrics began to experience a rebirth after the human appetite for drama had lain dormant for years. Acrobats and traveling minstrels visited towns and performed for audiences and jesters and singers were called upon to entertain at the feasts of rulers. The dramatic plays written by famous Greek poets were looked upon as texts rather than scripts. People of the Middle Ages read the works of the ancient poets but did not feel the need to bring them to life in the form of theatrical production which the authors had intended. Dramatic literature of the Middle Ages existed primarily in the form of the ancient scripts with no new dramatic literature matching the form created by the ancient Greeks.

Rise of drama:

The drama of the Middle Ages had its origins in religion, born of the Christian church. Whereas the church had outlawed ancient theatre as blasphemous, the new forms of drama were created by the church as a means of spreading its beliefs. In order to best relay the dialogues that occurred in the stories relating to Jesus's life, priests would each read the lines spoken by one character in the story.

Priests began acting out their lines to capture the interest of the congregation. These performances were common during Easter and the tradition soon extended to Christmas mass, where the Nativity story was retold through a theatrical production. The productions, however, began to grow into more elaborate and exaggerated tales that eventually bore little of the original intent. Priests could no longer exclusively handle the multitude of roles in a performance and were forced to invite laymen to participate. Eventually, the responsibility of these performances came to rest solely in the hands of laymen, who formed guilds and various organizations to handle each aspect of the productions.

English Cycles
The religious drama of the Middle Ages began as performances created by priests reenacting the stories of Jesus. The popularity of the productions grew to such an extent that the priests could no longer handle the various roles and the walls of the church could not accommodate the eager audiences. The productions were originally a unit portraying a certain episode in the life of Jesus or a saint. These units were eventually linked together to form a cohesive narrative called a *Cycle*. The Cycles could be broken into three main groups: Creation of man and the Old Testament, the Mystery of Atonement and the History of the Living Church. Old Testament plays tell of Adam and Eve in the garden, the corruption of mankind and the great flood. Atonement tells of the birth, life and sufferings of Jesus. The final Cycle tells of the lives of the saints, ministry of the apostles and of the Miracle of the Sacrament.

Morality plays
Near the beginning of the 15th century, the miracle plays of the Middle Ages gave way to plays of a different nature:

morality plays. The miracle plays, started at the hands of priests, were reenactments of episodes in the life of Jesus. As these plays grew in popularity, priests and churches could no longer accommodate the various roles or the space needed for such large-scale productions. Left to the guilds, the miracle plays began to evolve into plays that focused not on the life of Jesus, but on the lives of everyday people. These plays used allegory to teach a moral lesson. Characters in morality plays had names such as *Good Counsel*, *Pride* and *Avarice* and the role of the Devil was popularized. While these plays strayed from using religious figures as characters, the message maintained a religious tone: good men were religious men.

Medieval plays
Minstrels traveled from town to town in medieval days offering some source of entertainment. The minstrel often dressed in a festive costume as he wandered between towns on the back of a mule. Minstrels, accompanied by their harps, would sing about the saints, heroes and scripture at gatherings and feasts. Enthusiasts would often award the minstrel with gifts and tokens and the most talented minstrels were hired for permanent service by ruling kings and bishops. Minstrels served an important role, paving the way for the reintroduction of drama in the Middle Ages after Greek drama had been outlawed by the Christian church. As the popularity of minstrels increased, Paris became the headquarters of minstrelsy, allowing the minstrels to band together into groups that could command rights and privileges exclusive to their craft.

Origins of pantomime

The pantomime maintained a very indistinctive role in productions until English actor Joseph Grimaldi reinvented the pantomime clown role in Harlequin. Clowns, especially pantomimes, were a common character in many forms of theatre, and were generally portrayed as the servant of a more important character. Grimaldi had a talent for visual tricks and general buffoonery and brought clowns to life through his elaborate mechanical tricks. Actor John Rich, in 1717, played the role of Harlequin in the pantomime *Harlequin Executed*. Harlequin was originally a speaking part, but people like John Rich only used gesture, movement and facial expression to convey the same sentiments that had previously been expressed only through words.

Proletcult

Proletcult was the term given to the Russian movement of 1917, which aimed to create a form of art that was devoid of bourgeois influence. The intent of Proletcult Theatre was to create productions in which political propaganda was not the sole content and purpose. The Proletcult Theatre served to remind Russia's working class that they were subservient to an arrogant and often tyrannous upper-class. This form of theatre was also called *theatre of attractions* because it did not use plot-driven scripts, but instead employed random dynamic spectacles to shock the audience or solicit some other form of emotion.

Comedy of manners

Comedy of manners is a theatrical form credited to William Wycherley, George Etherege and William Congreve of 17th-century England, though Oscar Wilde rejuvenated the form in the 1890s. The comedy of manners is characterized by the distance between a society's selfish individual motives and simultaneous concern of projecting the image of being polite, well-mannered, educated citizens. This form of comedy became what is now known as Restoration Comedy. The style is characterized by its mocking of society and social norms and often targets marriage and love as the subjects of its mockery.

Origins of Elizabethan theatre

The story of Robin Hood was popularized in Tudor England by the companies of roving players. Productions were held in barns and inns as public theatre was poorly regarded by English government of the time. The government even attempted to stop the strolling players from performing in 1572 with the passage of laws forbidding the practice. There was concern that the performances were apt to incite rebellion among the population and that the players were escorting diseases such as the plague from town to town. Only actors hired by noblemen were allowed to perform and from 1572 to 1574 only four noblemen obtained license to begin theatre companies. As in Roman theatre, women were forbidden from participation and female roles were played by young boys. The popularity of the performances grew to such an extent that James Burbage, in 1576, built a theatre in London to accommodate the large audiences.

William Shakespeare's role
William Shakespeare is the most notable playwright of Elizabethan drama. Shakespeare's *Henry VI* was performed in 1592, followed by *Hamlet*, *Romeo and Juliet*, *The Merchant of Venice*, *King Lear*, *Julius Caesar* and *Macbeth*. Tudor audiences favored Shakespeare's plays involving the corrupt former kings of England and Elizabethan drama was both a source of entertainment and a podium

- 47 -

for political propaganda. Shakespeare's work was well-received by the masses because it appealed to all classes and all levels of education. His work drew upon both current and classical theories of the organization of the universe and man's place within it. Shakespeare's work was greatly influenced by the events of his time but it also maintained a universality that can be appreciated even today. Christianity was no longer the singular source of religion, the authority of Rome was in question and capitalism was on the rise. The replacement of classic ideas with more modern knowledge and thought made audiences all the more receptive to the works of Shakespeare.

Regulations imposed upon Elizabethan actors

In Elizabethan England, it was common for nobility to employ troupes of performers. These troupes began rapidly and some falsely claimed to be in the services of this or that lord. Members of false troupes were often beggars and vagabonds from whom nobility preferred to be distanced. In order to regulate the activity of false troupes, credentials were granted to credible performers and the aristocracy that maintained them. Elizabeth granted a royal patent, the first of its kind, to James Burbage and his four partners allowing them to perform anywhere in England. The only restriction was that political and religious subject matter could not be performed on stage, which led to objections by groups who had previously encouraged productions so long as they carried a religious message. In 1578 a total of six companies had a license to perform. In Elizabethan times, it was also the common practice for plays to be written by several authors with the actual owner being the company who performed the piece.

Restoration theatre

Restoration theatre is also known as the *comedy of manners*. For almost twenty years prior to the return of the Stuart dynasty in England, theatre was outlawed. Charles II, ruling king of England in 1660, greatly influenced by his earlier years in Paris, allowed two companies of players to begin performing while he ruled England. William Davenant was in charge of the Duke's Company while Thomas Killigrew ran the King's Company. During this time, women began to appear on stage for the first time. The most notable playwrights of Restoration comedy include William Wycherly, George Etherege and William Congreve. Popular themes of Restoration comedy included the comical nature of love and marriage.

Indian drama

Indian drama was born from an ancient tradition in which social and religious poetry was read at celebrations and feasts. According to Indian lore, theatre has mythical origins. The Indian culture believed there were three ages of man, each growing more distant from the will of the gods. According to this philosophy, humans began warring with each other, so the gods split the race into two sexes: men and women. The goal of the split was to create love; however, it only created desire for worldly things. Once the heart was drawn to outward desire, man lost his ability to be introspective. Pitying man's insatiable desires, the god Indra solicited the head god to create a spectacle so that humans could sate their appetite. The head god came up with the idea of Natya Veda or the Veda of the Theatre. Drama is the fifth Veda, a combination of the four earlier Vedas, which are dance, song, mimicry and passion.

India's indigenous drama

India's drama is unique in that its development was unaffected by foreign influence. Early European scholars held the view that Indian drama was originally an imitation of Greek drama but modern scholars know this to be untrue. The father of Indian drama, Bhrata, wrote many plays, thirteen of which exist today. The earliest one is dated 400 A.D. Indian plays had a unique structure in which they opened with a prayer followed by a narration of what was to come in the play. The narration would blend into the dialogue, giving way to the full performance. The majority of the plays' lines were in the form of prose in which beauty, morality and wisdom were described and reflected upon. Acts of violence and displays of affection were not part of Indian productions, though the plays did use stock characters such as the sneaky servant, the hero and the jester. Magic was the subject of many performances, having a character changed into an animal and requiring the intervention of the gods. The play would end with another prayer.

British theatre

Attack by Puritans

Elizabethan drama became a popular attraction for many citizens, but its value soon came into question by Puritanical minds. Beginning in 1622, the popularity of theatre declined rapidly, and by 1642, laws demanded that theatres be closed. Lawmakers believed that theatre was an unfit indulgence for the times and that the minds of citizens should be focused upon the political strife occurring within the country. A 1647 law threatened to imprison and punish anyone who attempted to violate the no-theatre laws, followed by another law declaring all actors vagabonds and requiring the demolition of any theatre-related equipment and buildings. During this time, actors who were found in violation of the laws were fined, whipped, stripped of clothing and imprisoned. It was not until the Restoration that theatre regained its footing in England.

Chinese drama

Chinese drama is rooted in and still holds true to religious tradition, relying heavily on the principles, superstitions and symbols of Taoism, Confucianism and Buddhism. The use of various combinations of these religious beliefs allow for Chinese dramatists to create extravagant productions often set in unearthly realms. While both Buddhism and Taoism provide a rich supply of symbolism, Confucianism is a much more intangible belief that centers on the worship of ancestors. Confucianist belief is most often represented in the musical theatre of the Chinese and Buddhist beliefs are often seen represented in acts of buffoonery towards gods and demons. The involvement of Chinese religion in theatre can be simplified in the following way: Confucianism involves morality, the dead past and worship of man; Buddhism involves idolatry, the changing future and worship of images; Taoism involves superstition, evils in the present and worship of spirits.

Symbolism

China is rich in national symbolism and this is reflected in its theatrical productions. Chinese drama views scenery as superfluous to a production, so it is implied through the words and actions of the actors. Lighting, also, is not an integral part of Chinese theatre. What the Chinese theatre lacks in scenery it makes up for in costumes, which are recreated accurately in the finest detail. The symbolism used in Chinese theatre is ancient and knowledge of its meaning has been handed down for generations, linking the past with the present. One such symbol is the *yin-yang*, which represents duality. Others are the dragon, a symbol of masculinity and heaven, and foxes, which symbolize deceit and trickery. Chinese drama also utilizes the sacred symbols known as the Hundred Antiques. These include the pearl, which prevents flood and fire; the coin, which signifies wealth; and jade, which brings justice. The Twelve Ornaments are also essential to Chinese theatre. These include images involving the sun, moon, dragon, birds and mountains.

Japanese drama

Noh plays, created by Kwanami Kiotsugu, were the dominant form of drama in 14th-century Japan. Noh plays, featuring only male actors, incorporated the use of masks for the parts of women or gods. This form of theatre is characterized by its rigid structure and unchanging tradition. The play always began with a traveler who reveals his own name and the destinations to which he will travel in the play. A chorus describes the scenery and the thoughts of the traveler as he wanders the stage. Each place the traveler visits is inhabited by the Spirit of the Place, a ghost that must tell a story of suffering. The ancient legend of the site is revealed through a combination of dialogue among actors and recitations from the chorus. The play ends as the traveler prays for the ghost to find peace and then a song is sung to honor the gods.

Kabuki
Kabuki theatre began in Japan in the late 16th century. In the Japanese Edo Era, there was a strictly observed distinction between the warrior class and the common people. It was during this era that kabuki theatre began to grow in popularity. Kabuki theatre addresses the injustices of the people faced with the harsh laws of the feudal system. Kabuki served as a means of expression for the merchant class, whose wealth surpassed that of commoners, but whose status was not part of the warrior class. Kabuki

began as a production in which the majority of players were female; however, due to concerns that the actresses were garnering undue attention, the government banned females from playing in kabuki performances in 1629. In kabuki theatre, female roles are played by males called *onnagata*. Kabuki is a unique form of theatre that combines several other types of Japanese theatre, taking inspiration from the Noh plays, puppet theatre (*bunraku*) and the realist productions of the 19th century.

Masques and Court Comedies

The theatre of the 16th century was divided into several groups, each suited to a particular class of people. *Court Comedies* were productions that were to be performed for the queen. Court Comedy was a variation on the popular pastoral drama form, many written by pastoral dramatist John Lyly. They were designed to sometimes subtly and other times overtly compliment Queen Elizabeth and the members of her court. Lyly's most notable work was the play *Endimion*, based upon the Greek myth of the shepherd named Endymion. Court *Masques* were introduced during the reign of Henry VIII in 1512. Players in masques were members of the king's court or even the royal family. Elaborate spectacles featuring music, costumes, scenery, mechanical effects and characters of mythological or allegorical origin, masques were limited to the private viewing by royalty as the performances were too costly to show in public theatres.

Commedia dell'arte
Commedia dell'arte, referring to improvisational drama, has its roots in Italy during the 16th and 17th centuries. These plays featured a scenario in which the characters were named and made aware of their relation to one another, the basic plot was outlined and the outcome

was predetermined. The scenario, or canvas, was the skeleton of the play and it was up to the actors to provide the flesh. The subject of this theatre form seemed to focus on the intrigues of love and clever schemes. There were several stock character types, usually identified by masks, including a sneaky servant, a group of old men, a lady's maid, a doctor, a captain or adventurer, a jester and a hunchback. Each character had a stock of phrases and gestures to be used during a performance in the event that they could think of nothing original to fill in the blank spaces.

Bavarian passion play

In the year 1634, the citizens of the Bavarian city Ober-Ammergau began a ritual performance of a passion play depicting the life and death of Jesus. The year before, a disease swept through southern Bavaria killing many of the inhabitants, though the valley of Ammer remained free of the illness. Authorities would not let anyone into or out of the city for fear of contracting the deadly disease. However, a resident wishing to return to the Ammer valley after working in a neighboring town managed to secretly gain entrance into the city. He brought the deadly disease with him, leading to his own death and to the deaths of one fourth of the city's population. The remaining citizens made a pledge to God that if He protected them from being wiped out by the plague they would perform a Passion Play every ten years depicting the life and death of Jesus Christ. The town's legend states that from that moment the infected citizens were cured and the town remained free of the disease.

Origins of Russian drama

Drama made its way into Russia by way of Poland in the 12th century. The plays were known as *Religious Dialogues* or *Histories*.

The performances were exclusive to monasteries until 1603 when they began to be performed in universities. The university performances were done in Polish or Latin, the earliest of which was a Latin piece entitled *Adam*, dated 1507, followed by a Polish piece entitled *The Life of the Savior from His Entry into Jerusalem*, which was dated 1533. While the origin of Russian drama is rooted in religious performances, Russia had a unique form of theatre called *the Vertep*. Vertep is a puppet theatre in which puppeteers control the dolls using strings attached to various parts of the doll. Vertep plays were used to depict religious stories. The word "Vertep" means "the secret place" and refers to the cave in which the Russian Orthodox Church believes Christ was born. Puppet characters include the Virgin Mary, Joseph, Jesus and various other figures central to the birth and life of Christ. Vertep plays eventually began to incorporate stories of a more secular nature.

Creation of opera

Opera, as a theatrical form, found its footing in 17th-century Italy. Musical science was a much sought-after field of study during this time in Italy. The Inquisition had limited the creative outlets in which previous artisans had found release. Music, however, remained one of the few forms of expression that the Inquisition allowed to exist. Poetry and literature began to decline and soon became secondary to the operatic form. Previous forms of drama, as they had been based on the Greek form, featured the dialogue of actors with a choral accompaniment in the background. In 1594 Italian poet Ottavio Rinuccini joined musicians Peri, Corsi and Caccini to create a piece in which this standard was reversed. The primary method of delivery became singing rather than dialogue and it became increasingly common for poets to write pieces specifically meant to be sung rather than spoken.

Origins of drama in Spain

The Spanish culture was known for its ballads, which translate well into a dramatic performance. The ballads of Spain contained legends that were introduced to the area from various locations. Spain's battle with the Moors had ended, but the culture of the Moors had left an imprint upon the Spanish. Travelers from countries north of Spain brought tales of chivalry, knightly quests and heroic tournaments. These stories, along with oriental influences, all made their way into the already popular Spanish ballads. The ballads became more and more elaborate, requiring multiple singers and detailed costumes and scenery. The addition of these elements transformed the ballad into full-blown dramatic productions. The works of both Lope de Vega and Calderon de Barca characterize Spanish drama at its height.

Origins of interludes, moralities and farces

Interludes, moralities and farces were all forms of drama that made an appearance in the Middle Ages. During this time, the classical definitions of comedy and tragedy did not apply. All that was required for a production to be a tragedy was the staging of a fight. The morality play was a religious performance that used allegory, featuring characters named after certain qualities that could be seen in men: Greed, Pride, Avarice and Patience. Interludes and farces were the more secular performances of the Middle Ages. They featured a variety of performers including pantomimes, strolling players and professional actors. Many of the performers had the ability to act, sing, juggle, perform acrobatics and do magic. Farces were most noted for comic situations that used characters to

which the audience could relate. Interludes were exactly what the name implies and were performed between acts of longer plays. Interludes, due to their brevity, were also commonly shown to entertain guests during celebrations and banquets.

Impact of Reformation on German drama

The Reformation was a catalyst of change all across Europe between 1517 and 1648. The movement began as an attempt to reform the Catholic church; however, it only managed to further divide the Christian sects. While the intentions of the Reformation were religious in nature, its ideas infiltrated all areas of society, including the theatre. Martin Luther, a German Protestant monk and major supporter of Reformation, supported theatre and believed that certain books of the Bible had been written as plays. He viewed theatre as a means for spreading religious truth. Luther approved of Christmas plays depicting the birth of Jesus but he banned Passion plays, as he did not agree with the portrayal of Jesus's suffering. During this time, every part of the Bible became eligible for depiction through drama. Clown-plays also began during this time. The clown-play, or Sottie, featured a costumed actor who told jokes to lighten the often somber mood of many plays. Sotties often occurred between acts of religious plays.

Origins of realism in Italian theatre

Realism made its debut in Italy following the fifty-year stint of Romanticism that began in 1852. Realism rejected the sentimental notion of the Romantics for a more practical view on life. Realists sought to examine the inner motives of the human being, desiring to use art as a means of depicting real life, as opposed to the Romantics, who used art to express what they wanted life to be like. Realists

- 52 -

rejected the Romantic idea that life was rational and emotionally fulfilling. Realism was an attempt to objectively portray life through various forms of art. While this modern way of thinking was drawing organized opposition in France, Germany and England, Italy had no mass of opposition. Certain small groups and outspoken individuals criticized realism, but there was no organized movement to protest it in Italy as there was in other countries.

Origins of vaudeville

The creator of *vaudeville*, Tony Pastor, was a professional circus clown. Vaudeville is a type of variety show involving various types of acts, usually unrelated to each other. They included singers, dancers, acrobats, comedians, animal acts, impersonators and magicians. These shows were originally exclusive to bars and dance halls until Tony Pastor altered the style to make it suitable for the stage. In order to achieve the level of success that Pastor wanted, he knew that he had to make the shows appeal to highly reputed citizens. Pastor rejected the lewd acts that were typical of vaudeville shows and banned drinking and smoking in the theatre where the shows were held. Edward Albee and B.F. Keith also played a large part in shaping the vaudeville theatre.

Position of actor

Profession
In the plays of ancient Greece, there were two distinct roles: an *actor* and *chorus members*. Chorus members were selected by a group called the *choregus*, while actors were chosen by the state. The title of "actor" only applied to the person in the play with the most prominent dialogue. Early Greek plays featured only one actor with the number increasing to three in the later years. While only a limited number were called actors,

several characters were present in plays, most of whom were silent or spoke only a few words. Before Aeschylus, the profession of actor was not distinct from that of poet because poets generally performed as actors. This distinction came about when Aeschylus introduced the second actor, meaning someone other than the poet was required to play a role in the production. In the early Athenian contests, only the poets received awards for their playwriting skills, but by the fifth century, awards were given to actors for their talents, thus turning acting into a distinct profession.

Social position
In ancient Greece, the status of the actor was elevated over time. In the fifth century B.C., acting became a profession and as such was viewed with great admiration and respect. Roman actors, however, had a much more contemptible social status. Playwriting was not a sought-after trade; rather, it was bestowed upon one by heredity. Actors were often slaves or foreign captives who were made to perform in exchange for their freedom. Many Roman rulers passed laws forbidding certain high-ranking officials from entering theatres or consorting with those who participated in the theatre. Women rarely appeared in Roman productions and those who did so were limited to roles as mimes.

Evolution of stage lighting

In its earliest days, theatre lighting was limited to the effects that could be harnessed from the sun, moon and stars. Early theatre was presented during daylight hours and the light that was cast upon the stage was controlled by nature. It can be assumed that theatre stages may have been built with this in mind. It is possible the stages were built in such a way as to cast shadows in the necessary places while positioning the most intense rays of light in others. Italian theatre began making use of candles for lighting effects in the 16th century: English theatre, in the 17th century. Oil lamps, in the 18th century, became the lighting method of choice. Gas lighting became available in the 19th century and the first theatre to use it was the Chestnut Street Theatre in Philadelphia. The first theatre to utilize electricity, discovered in 1879, was London's Savoy Theatre. In America, Boston's Bijou Theatre was the first to install electric lighting.

Time line of illumination techniques
Specific illumination, which became the preferred lighting method in the mid-19th century, involves a controlled shaft of light that can focus and highlight any part of the stage. The first form of specific illumination was the limelight, also called a *calcium light*, and was invented by Thomas Drummond. Arc lamps, powered by a battery, did not become a practical source of lighting until the invention of the generator. The invention of the incandescent spotlight soon replaced the arc light in theatres. The *baby lens*, invented by Louis Hartmann, was followed by Thomas Edison's invention of a concentrated filament for use in a spotlight. By the 1920s, spotlights were the predominant form of lighting.

Lighting designers

Adolphe Appia
The writing of Adolphe Appia is said to have given rise to modern lighting theory. Appia described three types of lighting in one of his plays: diffused light, creative light and painted light. He also identified four lighting cues: dazzling sunlight, the blood-red light of sunset, twilight and hazy darkness.

Norman Bel Geddes
Norman Bel Geddes, while best known for his impressive and large theatrical designs, also contributed to modern lighting techniques. Bel Geddes built a model theatre with an electric lighting system. He used this model to experiment with light sources and positions until he discovered the optimal combinations.

Robert Edmond Jones
Robert Edmond Jones, often referred to as the father of American scene design, used minimal scenery but dramatic lighting effects. One of his most memorable pieces was his staging of *Macbeth*. The entire performance took place on a bare stage with three giant moveable witch masks gazing down upon the performance. Jones used only single spotlights to isolate the acting areas.

Abe Feder:
Abe Feder, who studied at what is now Carnegie-Mellon University, was the first to coin the title "lighting designer." During his career, Feder was the lighting designer for over 300 Broadway shows. Feder was also known for his architectural lighting design, having created the lighting for the Empire State building, the RCA/GE building in Rockefeller Center and the United Nations building.

Jean Rosenthal
Jean Rosenthal is best known for her lighting design in musicals from the 1950s and 1960s. She is credited as the inventor of dance lighting.

Peggy Clark
Peggy Clark was the first female to hold the position of president in the United Scenic Artist organization. She assisted in scene design and was the lighting designer for several Broadway plays.

Adolphe Appia
Adolphe Appia shaped modern day stagecraft through his early theories involving staging, lighting and the use of space. He believed that space was a dynamic element that could be utilized to convey a much more realistic feel for

audiences. Appia began studying opera and soon decided that it did not offer the fluidity and staging that properly accentuated the human presence. He theorized that stage space would be better incorporated into a performance if it contained steps, ramps, platforms and drapes, all of which could be unified with actors through the use of lighting. Appia studied various operatic scenes in differing light and staging scenarios in order to find the best combinations. He published books on his theories, most notable of which are *The Staging of Wagner's Musical Dramas*, *Music and Stage Setting* and *The Work of Living Art*.

Contributors to theatre

Aeschylus, Sophocles and Euripides
Aeschylus, Sophocles and Euripides are considered the most famous Greek tragedians. Aeschylus is most noted for his trilogy called *The Oresteia*, which is comprised of *Agamemnon*, *The Libation Bearers*, and *The Eumenides*. Aeschylus became known as the father of Greek tragedy, since he pre-dated both Sophocles and Euripides. According to Aristotle, Aeschylus was responsible for changing the ancient form of the tragedy by adding a second actor, which diminished the participation of the chorus and focused on the dialogue. Sophocles, known for his work *Oedipus the King*, heightened the tragic form by adding a third actor and downsizing the chorus to fewer than fifteen members. Euripides was the first playwright to allow women to act in their tragedies.

History of Cleopatra
Since the time when the famous Queen of Egypt lived, her likeness has appeared in the dramatic productions of many artists. Samuel Daniel, in 1594, wrote a play entitled *Cleopatra*. In 1608, Elizabethan dramatist William Shakespeare wrote *Antony and Cleopatra*. John Fletcher and Francis Beaumont in their co-authored work, *The False One*, describe a Cleopatra much like the one found in Shakespeare's tale. In 1626, Thomas May wrote a play called *The Tragedy of Cleopatra, Queen of Egypt*. John Dryden's adaptation of Shakespeare's *Antony and Cleopatra* was entitled *All for Love*, featuring Cleopatra as a main character. American drama used Cleopatra as a central character in H. Rider Haggard's 1890 drama, *Cleopatra*. In 1899, famed comic dramatist George Bernard Shaw wrote a five-act play entitled *Caesar and Cleopatra*.

Contributions of Constantin Stanislavsky
German-born Constantin Stanislavsky is one of the most influential figures of the 20th century with regard to the acting process. He began acting at the age of 14 and as he got older moved to producing and directing. Stanislavsky's approach to acting was created over a forty-year period. He invented a method called the *Stanislavsky System*, which was at the forefront of modern psychological and emotional aspects of acting. His system became known as *the Method*. The fundamental principle of the Method is that it is the actor's primary responsibility to be believed. Method acting uses emotional memory. This approach was a novel idea in the acting world because it required actors to use parts of their own life, memories and personality while acting, whereas previous methods required actors to be blank slates, always ready to assume a new character's identity.

Lewis Carroll
Lewis Carroll is the pen name of Charles Lutwidge Dodgson, author of "Alice's Adventures in Wonderland" (1865), and its sequel "Through the Looking Glass" (1871). His literary reputation rests on these two children's books, although he wrote several other novels including "The Hunting of the Shark" (1876), "A Tangled Tale" (1885), and "Sylvie and Bruno" (1889). Carroll also wrote several

significant works on logic and mathematics. "Alice" was inspired by his favorite child-friend, Alice Liddell, and her two sisters to whom he related the story. Carroll was born in England in 1832 and became a mathematics teacher and resident Scholar of Christ Church College, Oxford. He assumed his pen name to protect his academic reputation that might be affected by authoring children's books. "Alice" brought him instant celebrity, and served as an entrée to Victorian society. Carroll remained at Oxford until his death in 1898.

Louisa May Alcott

Louisa May Alcott is one of America's beloved children's writer, novelist, and short-story writer. Alcott began her publishing career writing popular "dime novels" under pseudonyms to make a living. The publication of "Little Women" in 1868, and its huge popularity, allowed her to pursue serious fiction thereafter. "Little Women" is a fond narrative of family life based partially on her own family. It is a romantic, yet realistic novel with strong and memorable characters. Alcott's later novels include "Little Men" (1871) and "Rose in Bloom" (1876), both written for young readers. Her best adult fiction includes " Moods" (1864), a novel of married life, and "Work" (1874), a story based on her financial problems. Alcott was born in Boston in 1832 and reared in nearby Concord. Her father was the famous Transcendentalist thinker, Bronson Alcott. She died in 1888.

Mark Twain

Mark Twain, the pen name of Samuel Langhorne Clemens, was a true American voice in literature. Humorist, novelist, and travel writer, he is best known for "Tom Sawyer" (1876), and "The Adventures of Huckleberry Finn" (1884), beloved novels with memorable characters and undertones of social concern. "Life on the Mississippi" (1883) was an autobiographical account of his days on a riverboat. Twain's acid humor, and stories of a fading rural America, made him one of the most popular figures of his day. Born in 1835 in Hannibal, Missouri, Twain who was self--educated became a journalist and sometimes printer. His literary success made him a popular lecturer in America and Europe. His travels abroad provided Twain with the material for the satirical "A Connecticut Yankee in King Arthur's Court" (1889), and "The Innocents Abroad" (1869). His later life was marred by tragedy including the death of his wife and two daughters, as well as financial difficulty. He died in America in 1910.

Robert Louis Stevenson

Robert Louis Stevenson was a Scottish essayist, novelist, poet, and short-story writer. After writing for weeklies for a few years, his "Treasure Island" (1883) brought him acclaim and wealth. Stevenson followed this success with "Kidnapped" (1886), "The Strange Case of Dr. Jekyll and Mr. Hyde" (1886), and "The Master of Ballantrae" (1889), all critical and financial successes. Stevenson also wrote a book of verse for children, "A Child's Garden of Verses"(1885). His swashbuckling tales and colorful language engaged the fancy of the public, and he retired a wealthy man. Stevenson was born in Edinburgh in 1850 and was educated in law. His life was tainted by chronic tuberculosis, and he sought cures and more healthy climates all over the world. Stevenson finally found the relief he sought in Samoa, where he settled and lived the last years of his life. He died there in 1894, at the young age of 44.

Sir Arthur Conan Doyle

Conan Doyle's contribution to literature was the enigmatic detective, Sherlock Holmes. Conan Doyle based his character on a former professor at the University of Edinburgh. Holmes first appeared in 1887 in " A Study in Scarlet", and more

- 56 -

stories of the master of deductive reasoning appeared in magazines of the day. These stories were collected and published as "The Adventures of Sherlock Holmes" in 1892. Most memorable among the Holmes novels include "The Hound of the Baskervilles" (1902), " The Valley of Fear" (1915), and "The Sign of Four" (1890). Holmes also wrote a number of popular historical romances. Conan Doyle was born in London in 1859, and educated at Edinburgh. He trained as a physician and practiced medicine in Southsea from 1882-90. The success of his writing allowed him to largely retire from medicine.

Thomas Hardy

Hardy was an English novelist, playwright, and short-story writer. His dark works, often drawn from his own experience, include his first novel "Far from the Maddening Crowd" (1874), a tale of a strong woman and her three lovers. Hardy followed this modest success with four powerful novels, "Jude the Obscure" (1895), "The Return of the Native" (1878), "Tess of the D'Urbervilles" (1891), and "The Mayor of Casterbridge" (1896). All these volumes showcased Hardy's skills as storyteller and creator of strong characters. Hardy's poetry is also considered to be some of the best of his time. Hardy was born in Dorchester in Southwest England in 1840. Hardy was trained as an architect, which he gave up for writing when he achieved success. With death of his wife, Hardy was guilt ridden and his grief fueled the writing of his greatest poetry, "Poems of 1912-13". Hardy married again and lived until 1928.

William Hallam

William Hallam was a theatre actor-manager hailing from London. Hallam, recognizing America as rife with possibility for theatre arts, decided to create a company of players that he could send there. Hallam charged Robert Upton

with traveling to America and preparing theatres for his vision; however, Upton took the money Hallam gave him and joined another company of players in America, completely neglecting the mission for which he was sent. Despite losing the aid of Robert Upton, Hallam decided to continue as planned. William Hallam, while not the first to introduce drama to America, did much for establishing its permanence. He put together a company of players who had the talent to execute a variety of theatrical genres, thus allowing the company to offer a multitude of productions.

Lewis Hallam

Lewis Hallam came to America in 1753 with the acting company sent over by his brother William Hallam. Lewis and his wife were both members of this theatre company, which presented a signed testament of the members' ability and character from Governor Dinwiddie, the British advocate for colonial expansion in America. Despite the support of Dinwiddie, colonial magistrates refused to issue a license to Lewis Hallam for theatrical performances in New York. Hallam rousted public interest through petitions and was soon granted license to perform. He produced twenty-one plays during a six-month stay in New York, including comedies, tragedies and farces. Once the company had solidified itself in New York, the members decided to pursue similar fame in Philadelphia. Hallam faced the same reluctance from authorities in Philadelphia but soon managed to overcome them. Hallam remained in Philadelphia for two months before the company retired to the West Indies. It is here that Lewis Hallam passed away after a long illness. Hallam is credited as part of the original company that solidified the place of American theatre.

Eugène Ionesco

Romanian-native Eugene Ionesco is credited with creating the *theatre of the absurd*. Ionesco was born in 1909, but his family relocated to Paris, where he remained for sixteen years. In 1925, Ionesco returned to Romania with his father after his parents divorced. After a period of study, Ionesco wrote his first play in 1948. Ionesco's work rejected logical plots and standard character development. His plays were a comic portrayal of what he viewed as the absurdity of reality: man's existence as devoid of meaning in a universe ruled only by chance. Ionesco was attacked by critics for the lack of realism in his work and his rebuttal to these criticisms was that his writing was an effort to revitalize language and communication by saying things in a new way. People were shocked by Ionesco's views of drama and they either loved or hated it. In either case, talk of his work brought it increasing recognition. In 1962 Ionesco's niche in theatre history was defined by theatre critic Martin Esslin, who coined the term "theatre of the absurd" to describe Ionesco's work.

Henrik Ibsen
Norwegian native Henrik Ibsen is best known for bringing the French play to its height of perfection. Ibsen was not only a modern dramatist, but also a theatre manager and philosopher. Henrik Ibsen's work was prone to reflect his changing ideals. One work would proclaim the value of an ideal while in another work he would decry the selfsame value as worthless. He addressed this difference of opinion in his work titled *An Enemy of the People*, stating that most truths are obsolete after twenty years. His work further exposed what he saw as the social prejudices of his time. He extolled upon the value of the individual and each person's right to choose their own path in life. Ibsen believed that the true destiny of each man and the ultimate source of happiness was being true to one's self.

Ibsen's ideas were not well-received during his lifetime and he was attacked by other playwrights for his seemingly ridiculous ideas.

Jean Baptiste Poquelin de Moliere
In many circles Moliere, whose birth name was Jean Baptiste Poquelin, is considered one of the greatest comic dramatist of all time. The name *Moliere* was taken by the young Poquelin as a stage name but it soon became so popular that his original surname effectively ceased to exist. He was known for both writing and acting in many French satires that still exist today. Moliere's play titled *Tartuffe* is considered one of his most successful works. *Tartuffe* was first performed for Louis XIV but was attacked by 17th century censors, who managed to suppress the play for three years after its debut. Moliere trained in France and traveled with a company of actors for over twelve years developing his craft. Among his most notable works are *Don Juan*, *The Misanthrope* and *The Learned Ladies*. Moliere died during a stage performance after a coughing fit caused a blood vessel to burst.

Antonin Artaud
Antonin Artaud was a French poet, playwright, actor and director. Artaud aspired to create a form of theatre where actors would serve as an extension of the audience's most repressed realities. Artaud, who was a follower of the surreal movement, unfortunately suffered from mental problems and was hospitalized repeatedly throughout his lifetime. Most noted for his concept of the theatre of cruelty described in his book, *Theatre and its Double*, he believed that theatre needed to awaken people to the truths that they struggled to suppress in their daily lives. He rejected the idea that theatre could only exist as a story involving a character who, when faced with a problem, could find resolution by the end of the play. The cruelty Artaud

spoke of was not physical violence but a mental deliverance in which actors were presented as characters stripped of preconceived notions and outward appearances, the ultimate goal being to force audiences to see reality for what it was and not what others would have them believe it to be.

Voltaire
Francois-Marie Arouet was a famed French playwright during the Enlightenment. He was more commonly known by the name Voltaire, which he assumed following his first successful production in 1718. Voltaire, classically educated by Jesuit priests, was known for his rebellion against intolerance, which landed him in jail on multiple occasions. Voltaire was exiled from France for his radical views at the time and he sought refuge in England. He traveled to several places, including Brussels and Holland. One of Voltaire's earliest works, written when he was only 19, is *Oedipe*. The success of this play was followed by *Brutus, Zaire* and *Eriphile.* Voltaire is best noted for his use of exotic influence in his works. He used plot material from foreign lands including China and South America. Voltaire's works extended to works of poetry, prose and letter writing.

Gao Xingjian
Chinese-born dramatist Gao Xingjian was educated in the People's Republic with a love of theatre nurtured by his actress mother. His love of theatre and freethinking resulted in his incarceration in a re-education camp for six years. Under threat of persecution from Communist leader Mao Zedong, Gao Xingjian wrote in secrecy, believing that literature was a link to human consciousness. His works were not published until 1980 and in 1981 his plays were performed at the Beijing People's Art Theatre. His plays were influenced by Samuel Beckett, Antonin Artaud and Bertolt Brecht, causing his

work to be dubbed the "Chinese Theatre of the Absurd." Xingjian's play *Bus Stop* was based on Beckett's *Waiting for Godot*. *Bus Stop* was viewed as highly controversial and received much scrutiny from Communist Party authorities. Though the Chinese government could not accept the value of his work, Xingjian was awarded the Nobel Prize in Literature in 2000.

George Bernard Shaw
Irish-born socialist George Bernard Shaw authored over sixty plays in his lifetime, most of which was comedy but it always contained some form of social or political propaganda. Shaw claimed that the primary reason of high-writing was to sway the masses to his way of thinking. Shaw was considered a freethinker of the 20th century. He spoke out for women's rights and demanded equality of income. When he was awarded the Nobel Prize in 1925 for literature, he accepted the award but refused the money associated with it. Shaw's work was greatly influenced by Norwegian playwright Henrik Ibsen. In addition to being a dramatist, Shaw was a literary critic and an accomplished public speaker, especially as a spokesman for socialism.

Gordon Craig
Gordon Craig is credited with being one of the most influential faces of modern theatre. Craig's ideas on theatre can be seen in his 1904 book *The Art of the Theatre*. While many of Craig's peers believed that stage-directors should be merely interpreters, Craig saw the stage-director as a creator. It is a commonly held notion that the dramatist, director and actor align in a hierarchal form in which the actor is told what to do by the director, who is interpreting the words written by the dramatist. Craig believed that the role of the director superseded that of both the actor and the dramatist. He believed that theatre needed to be unified under the guidance of the

director. One of Craig's most controversial philosophies is that theatre can function independently of literature. He felt that impulses of the director or even the actor were sufficient to create a performance and that a script was not essential.

Richard D'Oyly Carte
Richard D'Oyly Carte is recognized as the manager of the Royalty Theatre in London, as well as the creator of English comic-opera. D'Oyly booked a short opera to be performed at the Royalty Theatre. In order to make the event longer in length, he hired W.S. Gilbert and Arthur Sullivan to write a one-act comic opera, which they entitled *Trial by Jury*. The performance was a huge success and D'Oyly booked many of Gilbert and Sullivan's productions in the various theatres he managed. Examples of comic-operas include *The Sorcerer*, *Patience* and The *Pirates of Penzance*. Carte also owned and directed multiple theatre companies in both England and America. Among the many theatre houses he owned in London were the Opera Comique, the Savoy Theatre, and the English Opera House, later to become the Palace Theatre. D'Oyly Carte was also a musical composer, creating such works as *Dr. Ambrosius: His Secret* and *Marie*.

Lope de Vega
Lope de Vega was a Madrid-born dramatist whose work is viewed as some of the best drama to come out of 16th- and 17th -century Spain. De Vega's work was characterized by his desire to place emphasis upon the individual. It is believed that de Vega's works were so popular that dramatists such as Voltaire, Shakespeare, Moliere and Marlowe all borrowed from de Vega's vast selection of writings. Lope de Vega's work consisted of four distinct styles: chivalrous drama, historical heroic drama, social life drama and sacred plays. It is believed that de Vega wrote near 2,200 plays in his lifetime, of which 481 exist today. Lope

de Vega created Spanish drama from the Spanish tradition, folklore and stories that were native to his country. He ignored the classical traditions of the ancient Greeks and created some of the first plays belonging to the genre of romantic drama.

Calderon de la Barca
Calderon de la Barca is best known for his ability to write both comic and tragic dramas. De la Barca, though he could write comedy, was most skilled with tragic drama. Much like Lope de Vega, de la Barca ignored the classical tradition of writing and instead drew material from the stories and culture of his native land. Of the hundreds of plays that have been credited to de la Barca only 181 have been proven authentic. His work often featured supernatural themes, grim humor and innovative plots. Much of de la Barca's work was influenced by his devout Catholicism just as much of his work was limited by his refusal to accept modern thinking. He was deeply medieval in his beliefs and resisted modern ideas, yet he still managed to produce some of the best romantic dramas of 17th-century Spain.

George II, Duke of Saxe-Meiningen
The Duke of Saxe-Meiningen has been dubbed the first modern director. His works influenced theatrical pioneers including actor/manager Andre Antoine Konstantin Stanislavski. George II was known for designing his own sets, training his actors and conducting every rehearsal. The Duke paid special attention to details and planned each moment of each scene. He preferred to have stage props such as chairs, chimneys and doors that were real rather than drawn or created. The Duke created his own design rules, exemplified by his utilization of steps and levels to divide the stage into separate areas. . He refused to set anything in the middle of the stage, believing that a pleasing visual

- 60 -

composition was one in which the middle of the picture was not centered on the middle of the stage. He also used various natural materials such as tree branches to hide technical equipment above the stage. In order to craft the most effective production, the Duke felt it was necessary to observe all movements on stage from visual and acoustic perspectives of various audience positions.

Vsevolod Emilevich Meyerhold

Russian-born Vsevolod Emilevich Meyerhold performed the roles of actor, director and producer during his lifetime and was known for his socialist tendencies. He studied law for a short time, but soon abandoned law school for the Moscow Philharmonic Dramatic School, which was co-founded by Konstantin Stanislavski. Meyerhold went on to act in and direct several productions, each of which served as an opportunity for him to experiment with staging methods. He incorporated symbolism into most of his work because he believed it was a crucial part of any dramatic production. Stanislavski despised Meyerhold's work and wanted nothing to do with his work. One of Meyerhold's goals was to reinvent Commedia dell'arte in a more contemporary style. Meyerhold's acting technique was in direct opposition to Stanislavski's method. Meyerhold believed that emotion could be conveyed through use of practiced postures and gestures regardless of the actor's actual emotional state.

David Belasco

American-born David Belasco was a playwright, director and producer who got his start in theatre in San Francisco, where he was born. He worked as script copier and callboy in various theatres until his playwright skills were noticed. He then moved to New York and became a stage manager for the Madison Square Theatre before becoming an independent producer in 1859. His most notable works are *Madame Butterfly* and *The Girl of the Golden West*. Belasco wrote, directed or produced most of the plays shown on Broadway between 1884 and 1930. He also furthered naturalism in the theatre by using unconventional methods, such as placing scents in air ducts in the theatre to heighten the reality of a scene. He used working washing machines and dryers in his productions and his actors would cook real food if the script called for scenes involving eating. Belasco's attention to detail also gave rise to some advanced lighting techniques, which he used to create a mood or evoke a certain setting.

Roman playwrights

Titus Maccius Plautus and Publius Terenius Afer

Both Plautus and Afer wrote comic plays. Their work, in fact, is the only surviving comic drama of the ancient Roman theatre. Plautus' work was very popular in his lifetime. His most notable works include *Pot of Gold*, *The Menaechmi* and *Braggart Warrior*. Like all Roman theatre, Plautus' comedy was based on the Greek New Comedies. He added allusions familiar to Roman culture as well as Latin dialog and poetic meters. Afer, who was better known as "Terence," was a freed Roman slave. The six plays he wrote that survive today are *Andria*, *Hecyra*, *Heautontimoroumenos*, *Eunuchus*, *Phormio*, and *Adelphi*. His plays used more complex plots, intriguing characters and even double-plots. The language used by Terence was more elegant than that of Plautus' plays, though Terence did not achieve the same popularity that Plautus did.

Freie Bühne

Freie Bühne is a German phrase meaning free theatre. The Freie Bühne was a German society in Berlin that sponsored performances that were banned or censored by commercial theatres. The origins of the society coincide with the visitation of Paris' Théâtre Libre to Berlin. Otto Brahm, theatre critic and proponent of naturalism, was part of the group that formed to create the society. One of the first works the society sponsored was Henrik Ibsen's *Ghosts. Vor Sonnenaufgang*, written by Gerhart Hauptmann, was the second play performed. This production was the first naturalistic play to be performed in Germany, relating a tale of a family's downfall at the hands of alcoholism, corruption and desire for wealth. The society ceased to exist in 1893 after only four years.

Major names in theatre

Alfred Bunn was an English theatrical manager who managed London's Drury Lane Theatre, Birmingham's Theatre Royal and London's Convent Garden. He also attempted to establish the opera in England.

James Burbage, an English actor, erected the first theatre in London called The Theatre in Shorditch and started the Blackfriar's Theatre.

Christopher Marlowe was famed for his blank verse. Marlow's plays include *Tamburlaine, Doctor Faustus* and *The Jew of Malta* He was an Elizabethan dramatist who preceded Shakespeare, a poet and a fictional writer.

William Congreve, an English dramatist, was famed for his comic dramas.

Gao Xingjian created what is known as the Chinese *Theatre of the Absurd*. Xingjian won a Nobel Prize for Literature in 2000.

John Heywood, English dramatist, transformed morality plays from the Middle Ages into modern productions by changing the allegorical characters into real people.

John Lyly brought the pastoral to England and created the form of Court Comedy.

Ben Johnson, a London-born dramatist, was famed for works of comedy and satire.

Hans Sachs was a German shoemaker, writer, singer and songwriter. He wrote over 208 plays during the 16th century.

Lope de Rueda was a Spanish actor, manager and playwright who invented the Spanish version of the short farce called *pasos*.

Emile Zola was a French writer who supported naturalism.

Honore de Balzac was a French writer who is credited as the founding father of realism in European literature.

Henry Becque was a 19th-centuryFrench playwright who incorporated both naturalism and realism into his work.

Aphra Behn was the first female English playwright and a British spy.

Major playwrights

Ionesco: Rhinoceros, The Chairs, The Bald Soprano, The Lesson, The Killer, Exit the King, Hunger and Thirst and A Stroll in the Air.

Shaw: Pygmalion, Caesar and Cleopatra, Androcles and the Lion, The Doctor's Dilemma, Candida and Major Barbara.

Marlowe: Tamburlaine, Doctor Faustus, The Jew of Malta, Edward II and The Massacre at Paris.

Congreve: The Way of the World, The Old Bachelor, Love for Love, The Double-Dealer and The Mourning Bride.

Xingjian: Absolute Signal, Wilderness Man, Between Life and Death and Dialogue.

De Vega: The Star of Seville, The Sheep Well, The Foolish Lady and Punishment Without Revenge.

De la Barca: Devotion of the Cross, Life is a Dream and The World is a Fair.

Ben Johnson: The Alchemist, Every Man out of His Humor, The Sad Shepherd, The Masque of Blackness.

Hans Sachs: Lucretia, Virginia.

Lope de Rueda: Eufemia, Medora, Armelina.

Giovanni Verga: The She-Wolf, In the Porter's Lodge, The Wolf Hunt, The Fox Hunt, and Rustic Chivalry.

J. M. Barrie: Peter Pan, Mary Rose, What Every Woman Knows, Quality Street, The Admirable Crichton.

Pierre Beaumarchais: The Barber of Seville, The Marriage of Figaro.

Samuel Beckett: Waiting for Godot, Endgame, and Happy Days.

Bertolt Brecht: Baal, A Man's a Man, The Threepenny Opera, The Life of Galileo, Mother Courage, The Caucasian Chalk Circle, The Visions of Simone Machard.

Anton Chekhov: The Seagull, Uncle Vanya, The Cherry Orchard, and The Three Sisters.

George Cohan: Seven Keys to Baldplate, The Little Millionaire, Little Nelly Kelly, and Forty-five Minutes from Broadway.

Richard Brinsley Sheridan: The Rivals, The Critic, A Trip to Scarborough, and The School for Scandal.

Friedrich von Schiller: The Robbers, Don Carlos, Maria Stuart.

Johann Wolfgang von Goethe: Faust, The Lover's Caprice, Clavigo, Egmont, Stella, Iphigenia in Tauris, Torquato Tasso.

Theatre of the Absurd

Theatre of the Absurd, also called *New Theatre* and *anti-theatre*, is a phrase brought into existence by drama critic Martin Esslin. Esslin wrote a book bearing this title in 1962 addressing the type of play in which the human condition is decried as meaningless. The view of man's meaninglessness in the universe was a philosophy born of the Frenchman Albert Camus. Camus claimed that man had to resign himself to the fact that the universe defied logical explanation and could only be seen as absurd in its behavior. Esslin identified Eugene Ionesco, Samuel Beckett, Jean Genet, Arthur Adamov and Harold Pinter as the five defining playwrights of the absurdist movement. While this form of theatre was only recently assigned its own title, absurdist elements can be noticed in works as far back as those of Aristophanes. Absurdist elements can be identified in most plays predating the definition of Theatre of the Absurd, including Medieval morality plays and Elizabethan dramas. World War II, it is thought, readied the minds of playgoers for the themes presented in the Theatre of the Absurd.

Claque in French theatres

The *claque* was an organized group of people hired to applaud during theatrical performances. The idea is believed to have originated when the emperor Nero required that five thousand soldiers chant his praise after a performance. Sixteenth-century poet, Jean Daurat, used this ancient practice as the foundation for the formation of the claque. "Claque" is derived from the French term "claquer," meaning to clap one's hands. Daurat's idea to ensure applause for performances was to give free tickets to any patrons who agreed to show their approval of the show. Eventually this practice became so popular that there developed a professional organization for claquers. In 1820 a man by the name of Sauton formed a business that supplied claquers to playwrights. It was the responsibility of the theatre manager to request the number of claquers necessary for a performance. The duties of the claquers reached beyond simple clapping. They could laugh at jokes, fake tears, encourage encores and generally ensure the audience remained happy.

Superstitions involving theatre

Theatrical participants ranging from managers to actors, even today, hold some of the same superstitions that originated in the early years of theatre. One such superstitious belief is that blue scenery robs actors of wealth or lead to death. Blue scenery, in early European theatre, was allowed only if silver ornaments were hung, as silver was believed to ward off evil. Another superstition warns that Sunday rehearsals ensure disaster for actors and patrons. This arose from the death of New York's Grand Opera House manager after he called for a Sunday rehearsal. Another belief is that on the opening night of a new play, the first person admitted cannot be the holder of a free ticket or the play will fail. The black cat is seen as a sign of good fortune in theatres, while peacock feathers are renowned as bad luck. The luck in carrying a rabbit's foot led early actor Edmund Kean to dig up the remains of a deceased actor and procure one of his toe bones, to which Kean later attributed his great success.

Origins of American theatre

American theatre is believed to have originated early in the 18th century. The state of Virginia is recognized as the place in which American theatre first originated based on the 1716 construction of a theatre in Williamsburg. The New England provinces housed some of the earliest public theatres on record, despite their reputation for abhorrence of the theatre. The North as a whole seemed to view theatrical performances with much more contempt than their neighbors to the South. Few records exist relating to early American plays as a result of the multitude of laws passed prohibiting the performance or advertisement of such productions. Even with laws forbidding theatre, records of theatrical performances indicate that plays existed as early as 1702 in America.

George Farquhar's comedy *The Recruiting Officer*

The Recruiting Officer holds a place in American history as the earliest play presented in New York of which a record exists. The play took place at the New Theatre in New York on December 6, 1732. The New Theatre was in a building that was owned by the city's acting governor, Rip Van Dam. The cast was composed of a group of actors who are believed to have come to America from London for the purpose of acting. The play itself, written by Irish-born George Farquhar, was written in London at a time when the town's recruiting officers were busy signing citizens into the military. The play had an overall witty tone and the dialogue was often bordering on indecent and raunchy by modern standards.

Analyzing and interpreting a script

A director must analyze a script in order to gain an understanding of the text's overall structure and theme. The director must carefully study the function of each character in the script. Once they understand the hierarchy of the characters, they must consider how that will translate into demands for the actor. The director must consider the script's technical requirements, including lighting, costumes and sound. The director must take into consideration the time period in which the play was written compared to the time period in which the script takes place. Directors must be able to read the script and gather information regarding the context and subtext of the work. It may also be helpful for a director to understand the biography of the playwright as well as be familiar with some of their other works.

Tone and impact
When reviewing a script, a director must identify several elements to determine, given his resources, whether the script is suitable for performance. Directors look for certain details in the script that lend to the overall tone of a performance and

they must identify the elements in the script that will bring the play to life. Ranking the importance of each element and determining if the overall tone of the play would be strengthened or weakened by manipulating those elements is also important. These elements include light, sound, setting, props, language and costumes. It is easy to manipulate these elements, since character, idea, and story are integral to the story and should generally remain unchanged. The director should identify the peaks of excitement in a script and build upon these to bring energy and dynamic structure to the play.

Script analysis

Beckerman believed that a play script was like a musical score. Musical scores indicate the sounds that are played by a human or instrument, whereas a script indicates the shape of the energy that is to be expressed by a person. Beckerman identified and termed many elements of a script. He referred to the person exerting energy as the "impelling agent." The impelling agent exerts energy in an effort to achieve a goal, which Beckerman terms the "project." The impelling agent encounters many obstacles in pursuit of the project and Beckerman terms these obstacles "resistance." Beckerman also believed that a play should be broken into units which he called segments. Each segment consists of an impelling agent overcoming resistance to complete a project.

The Dynamics of Drama
Beckerman's method of script analysis, when first introduced, was different from all other approaches. The standard script analysis required one to identify the elements of a script including character, plot, setting and theme. This method forced the interpreter to view the play from the outside as though all of its parts existed simultaneously, but this is not the manner in which a play is performed or

viewed. Beckerman reasoned that this should not be the way a script is analyzed. Rather, his method of analysis requires that the script be broken into units called "segments." In each segment the impelling agent completes a project. The project may be as simple as exerting energy that helps actors/characters psychologically adjust to the changes around them.

Active and reactive segments
In Bernard Beckerman's book *The Dynamics of Drama* he states that script analysis should involve breaking a script into segments. Each segment consists of an impelling agent exerting force to overcome resistance, resulting in the completion of a project. A segment can be termed "active" if the agent is exerting force externally. Active segments are goal-oriented and require the agent to perform an action to complete the project. A "reactive" segment is produced when an agent must exert energy internally in order to emotionally or psychologically adjust to a change. Reactive segments generally consist of an agent who experiences a change rather than creates one.

Crux and decrescence
Beckerman's treatment of script analysis requires that the script be broken into segments. Each segment consists of an impelling agent exerting energy to overcome resistance resulting in the completion of a project. Segments may be active or reactive depending on the type of energy the agent is required to exert. In each segment there is a point at which it becomes clear whether the resistance or the project will be the prevailing force. This point is called the *crux*. The crux is the point at which a dramatic shift of power occurs between the resistance and the project. Each segment ends in what is called the *decrescence*. The decrescence is the change or reaction to the change that has been brought about by the crux. The decrescence is the agent's response to the

prevalence of either the resistance or project.

Analyzing characters

There are three types of objectives: objective, super-objective and sub-objective. The objective in the most general sense is the character's goal. In order to best analyze a character one must be able to interpret what the script says directly and, even more importantly, what it says indirectly. One should be able to infer information about the character being analyzed from the choices the character makes, the relationships the character has and what other characters say and think about the character being analyzed. The basic objective is the character's goal in each scene. When analyzing a character, one should read the script with the intention of discovering what the character wants to accomplish in each scene. The super-objective is the character's goal for the whole play. It may also be called the *spine* or *through line.* The sub-objectives are small changes in a scene involving mood, subject and intention. Each of these objectives should be identified when analyzing a character.

Subtext:

According to teacher, director and writer Robert Cohen, acting is the process of effectively interpreting and conveying the subtext in relationships between characters. He created the term "relacom" to refer to the communication in a relationship. When analyzing a character one should consider the overt characterization as well as the subtle characterization that is inferred from a character's body language, motives and interaction with other characters. It is important to understand what a character says but is just as important to understand the way it is said. The manner in which a character says things conveys the underlying meaning of the thoughts and actions behind the dialogue. Subtext is an important part of understanding a character, as it can define the identity of a character or clarify a relationship with another character. Subtext is often the key in developing an effective and believable character.

Production meeting

A production meeting is often held after the play is selected. It can occur before and/or after the actors or selected. The actors can be a part of the meeting or not depending on the director. This meeting allows the director to meet with the theatre staff and technicians to determine how the production will be laid out. The director relays his vision to the set designers, being careful to do so in a manner that will allow the designers the freedom to interpret and create the layout themselves. It is important for the director to provide a focus for the group while allowing each member to contribute in their unique way. The director can elaborate upon his vision and clarify what his exact needs are for the production. The group provides feedback on what they can or cannot do based on the director's expectations.

Staging a play

Staging a play is the process of determining where actors should physically be located at various points in the play. The aim of this exercise is to ensure that the position of the actors achieves the desired visual focus. The actors, props, set and lighting need to all work together to focus the audience's attention to the right place at the right time. Staging a play also involves blocking, which is pinpointing where the actors should be situated on stage. Staging a play also involves coordinating stage business, which is any activity that takes place on stage during a performance. For example, an actor may answer a telephone as part of a scene.

Stage positions

Actors and directors should be familiar with the various stage positions that best achieve visual focus. It is important for the stage to be set up in an appropriate manner so that the audience can focus on the action occurring on stage. Actors can use body positions to gain the audience's attention. A full front position or center stage automatically warrants the audience's attention. On stages that have multiple levels built into the set, an actor who stands at the highest level will hold the most visual focus. On a flat stage, the actor who stands farthest downstage, which is closest to the audience, will hold the most visual focus. If multiple actors are on stage they can be arranged in a triangular pattern with the actor at the apex of the triangle receiving the most visual focus. Actors can also be separated from the group by contrast. For example, if one actor on stage is standing while the rest are seated, the standing actor receives the visual focus.

Body positions

Full front is a position in which the actor faces the audience exposing the entire front of the body. It is an open position that allows the actor to be fully seen and heard by the audience. Open positions are those in which the actor's face, at the very least is facing the audience. Quarter (¼) right and left positions are those in which the actor stands facing slightly left or right of the audience. Quarter positions are open positions. Quarter positions allow two actors to be on stage interacting with each other naturally while still allowing the audience to hear and see them. Left and right profiles are positions in which the actor exposes only one side of their face and body to the audience. Profiles are not open positions and drastically reduce the visibility of the actor to the audience. In between the profile and quarter positions are the three-quarter (¾) right and left positions. These are not quite profiles. Opposite of full front is the full back position. In full back position the actor faces away from the audience.

Staging terms

A *cross* is a stage direction given by the director. It means the actor needs to move from one point on stage to another. For example, a director may instruct the actor to cross stage right. In a script, instructions to cross the stage are often shown by the letter "x." A direction to counter-cross is given in order to compensate for the cross of another actor. In order to retain a visual balance in a scene, the director may instruct one actor to cross stage right while instructing another actor to counter cross in order to avoid being blocked from view by the crosser. In general, if there are two actors on stage, each is of equal importance. If one actor steps farther away from the audience (or upstage), it causes an awkward interaction between the actors. The actor who has been upstaged must then turn his back to the audience in order to look as though he is naturally communicating with the other actor; however, this means the audience will not be able to hear the actor speaking. Upstaging should be avoided.

Research

Research is a means of critical inquiry, investigations based on sources of knowledge.

- Research is the basis of scientific knowledge, of inventions, scholarly inquiry, and many personal and general decisions. Much of work consists of research - finding something out and reporting on it. We can list five basic precepts about research.
- Everyone does research. To buy a car, go to a film, to investigate anything is research. We all have experience in doing research.

- Good research draws a person into a "conversation" about a topic. Results are more knowledge about a subject, understanding different sides to issues, and being able to intelligently discuss nuances of the topic.
- Research is always driven by a purpose. Reasons may vary from solving a problem to advocating a position, but research is almost always goal oriented.
- Research is shaped by purpose, and in turn the fruits of research refine the research further.
- Research is usually not a linear process; it is modified and changed by the results it yields.

Heretical approach to directing

According to the heretical approach to directing, the director's job is to interpret the script to create a dramatic production that will be enjoyed by an audience. The director must work to make a script exciting to the audience. This approach requires that directors interpret the script, maintaining its overall meaning while exercising creative freedom to alter an ending or omit certain scenes. This approach can be seen in classical works that are translated to opera. English-born doctor Thomas Bowdler used this approach to rewrite the works of Shakespeare, omitting what he saw as offensive or unsuitable parts. He called his book *The Family Shakespeare*, as he believed he had transformed Shakespeare's work so that a father could read it to his children without fear of corrupting them. Directors may use this approach, though it is most often associated with a prudish censorship that does not lend itself to the theatre.

History of directing
In ancient Greece the modern director's role was performed by a *choregus*. The choregus was the leader of the chorus and it was his job to direct and coordinate songs and movements. In ancient Roman theatre, productions were organized by a wealthy patron who provided the financing necessary for a performance. In medieval times, the role most closely related to that of the modern director was called the "master of secrets." The master of secrets was responsible for special effects and because of the detail and coordination required to perform these effects successfully and safely, he was essentially responsible for telling actors where to stand. In the period when actors had to register in order to perform, the director role was carried out by the keeper of the register. The register was an official copy of a script that was performed by a specific theatre company. The keeper of the register was usually a guild, or group of craftsmen, who were responsible for maintaining the integrity of the script by handing it down to each successive generation.

Modern role of director
Directors perform both artistic and managerial roles. The modern theatre director must interpret a script, cast actors, design the production, conduct rehearsals and coordinate a vast number of other tasks and elements. Oftentimes, interpreting a script requires the director's use of creative license. Directors must master human relations, as they work with actors, set designers and lighting crews to bring a script to life. Directors must be capable of making quick decisions while being able to adapt to change. Directors often act as business managers, publicity directors or even costume designers and they are skilled at working with the resources they have available to unify the various elements that comprise a dramatic production.

Coaching actors
Due to the work of Konstantin Stanislavsky, it is now common for

directors to collaborate with actors in order to create a successful performance. Directors can be encouraged to guide actors but should also be cautioned not to over-direct actors. This could lead to dependency, so it is usually best for the direct to consult with the actor rather than instruct the actor. The director can be an advisor or a source of inspiration and encouragement for an actor. The actor and director each must recognize the other's creative talents and work together to incorporate their visions into a unified performance that leaves both parties, and the audience, feeling satisfied. The way in which the director cooperates with the actor can take many forms. Sometimes the director will assume one role and maintain it or perhaps fluctuate among different roles. Examples of these roles include the *authoritarian*, the *visionary* and the *therapist*.

Managerial responsibilities

One of the many aspects of the director's role is that of manager. The director must serve both in an artistic capacity when interpreting a script and in a managerial capacity when organizing and coordinating the details of a performance. The director must handle scheduling, casting and rehearsals as well as conduct read-throughs in which the director and actors read the script and discuss their vision for the characters and design of the play. The director leads rehearsals, which can occur with all actors present to rehearse the entire play or with only a few actors rehearsing a portion of the play. The director leads run-throughs, technical rehearsals and dress rehearsals and may even conduct previews which involve executing a performance outside of the intended venue in order to discover any areas of the performance that need to be worked out before opening. The director's job is usually ends after opening night, at which point the stage manager takes over.

Brainstorming

Brainstorming is a technique used frequently in business, industry, science, and engineering. It is accomplished by tossing out ideas, usually with several other people, in order to find a fresh approach or a creative way to approach a subject. This can be accomplished by an individual by simply free-associating about a topic. Sitting with paper and pen, every thought about the subject is written down in a word or phrase. This is done without analytical thinking, just recording what arises in the mind about the topic. The list is then read over carefully several times. The writer looks for patterns, repetitions, clusters of ideas, or a recurring theme. Although brainstorming can be done individually, it works best when several people are involved. Three to five people is ideal. This allows an exchange of ideas, points of view, and often results in fresh ideas or approaches.

Freewriting

Freewriting is a form of brainstorming in a structured way. The method involves exploring a topic by writing about it for a certain period of time without stopping. A writer sets a time limit, and begins writing in complete sentences everything that comes to mind about the topic. Writing continues without interruption until the set period expires. When time expires, read carefully everything that has been written down. Much of it may make little or no sense, but insights and observations may emerge that the free writer did not know existed in his mind. Writing has a unique quality about it of jogging loose ideas, and seeing a word or idea appear may trigger others. Freewriting usually results in a fuller expression of ideas than brainstorming, because thoughts and associations are written in a more comprehensive manner. Both techniques can be used to complement one another and can yield much different results.

Figurative language

Poetry is a genre in which language is used in all its variations and embellishments to convey a sense, mood, or feeling the poet deems important. Poetry uses elaborate linguistic constructions to explain the world in creative ways. Poetry manipulates language itself to convey impressions in new and innovative constructions. It makes extensive use of figurative devices such as conceits, similes, metaphors and many more to express things in fresh ways. These devices will be treated separately later. Together, poets use figurative language to suggest rather than give direct meanings. This language provides a creative experience for the reader who is asked to understand meaning in unconventional terms. Poets relish the opportunities to express themselves in creative and unusual words. Figurative language provides both poet and reader an opportunity for unique expression and understanding. Emotions, feelings, and moods are invoked by the skillful use of figurative language.

Hyperbole

Hyperbole is a figure of speech that uses extreme exaggeration for dramatic effect. It usually functions to compare and is used quite often in romantic works. Love poetry is an example of a subgenre that fosters the use of hyperbole. Hyperbole may also be used in a farcical manner for comic effect.

Personification

Personification is another figure of speech, which attributes human qualities to an inanimate object or abstract entity. Personification helps us to use our self-knowledge and extrapolate it to understand abstract concepts, forces of nature, and common events. Personification is sometimes achieved by similes or analogies to strengthen the imagery.

Foreshadowing

Foreshadowing uses hints in a narrative to let the audience anticipate future events in the plot. Foreshadowing can be indicated by a number of literary devices and figures of speech, as well as through dialogue between characters. In Ibsen's play "Hedda Gabler", Hedda plays with a gun early in the play, which foreshadows her eventual suicide. In Shakespeare's "Macbeth", the three witches in the opening scene foreshadow horrific events to come. Examples abound in all forms of literature, but are perhaps most evident in drama.

Allusions

An allusion is a reference within a text to some person, place, or event outside the text. Allusions that refer to events more or less contemporary with the text are called topical allusions. Those referring to specific persons are called personal allusions. An example of personal allusion is William Butler Yeats' reference to "golden thighed Pythagoras" in his poem "Among School Children". Allusions may be used to summarize an important idea or point out a contrast between contemporary life and a heroic past. An example of this would be James Joyce's classical parallels in "Ulysses" in which heroic deeds in the "Odyssey" are implicitly compared to the banal aspects of everyday life in Dublin. Allusions may also be used to summarize an important idea such as the concluding line from "King Kong", "It was beauty killed the beast". A writer may use allusions as literary devices to achieve a number of dramatic effects as noted above.

Style of literature

In literature, style is a particular manner of using language to narrate a story, develop a dramatic mood, or evoke a mood. Style can also refer to a period of literary history or to an individual writer.

Tone:
Tone refers to the attitude expressed about the subject through the author. This expression is communicated by language, character development, plotting, and the creation of attitudes about the subject. Mood is sometimes mistaken for tone, but the two have important differences. Mood is generally understood to be the feeling the work provokes in the audience. Although this can sometimes be identical to tone, they are often quite different.

Diction:
Diction is the choice of language in a literary work. Diction may be formal, colloquial, or slang. The use of diction to set a tone for the work is meant to induce a mood in the audience. Slang is used commonly in modern fiction while formal and colloquial diction are used for specific effects.

Characters

A protagonist is the central character in a play or story. The character opposing the protagonist is called the antagonist. Either may be the hero or villain of a drama or work of fiction. In modern literature the protagonist-antagonist struggle is often represented as an internal conflict in one individual. Freudian thought has had a great influence on this inward battle of psychological forces in a person. The hero or heroine is also the major figure in a literary work. The term may be used instead of protagonist. Finally, the villain is the major evil character in a literary work. Usually the villain opposes the protagonist but sometimes is the protagonist of a work. The roles of heroes and villains are exaggerated in melodrama and often seen in early films. The conflict in these cases usually involves a "fair damsel". Modern literature usually reflects a more mixed character, with both qualities present in a character.

Plot development

Climax
A climax occurs when a state of tension in a literary work reaches its peak, usually with a resolution of some kind. There may be many or only one climax in a work, depending on the plotting and length of the story. A climax is usually preceded by an increasing level of tension, usually between the protagonist and antagonist. The climax may take the form of action, speech, or symbolism.

Anticlimax:
An anticlimax occurs in fiction or drama when a critical point in the work is resolved and the dramatic tension recedes. The term can be used negatively if it refers to a weakness in a drama or story. Sometimes an anticlimax is used to enhance a scene or serve as a respite from a period of action.

Closure:
Closure is the modification of the structure of a work, which makes absence of further development unlikely. It creates the expectation of nothing and leaves the reader or audience satisfied that the plot development is over. Closure often has a dramatic force of its own and sometimes is the final climax.

Syllogism

Deductive reasoning is constructed in a three-step method called a syllogism. The three steps are the major premise, the minor premise, and the conclusion. The major premise is a generalization, and the minor premise is a specific case. The conclusion is deduced from applying the generalization to the specific case. Deductive arguments fail if either the major or minor premise is not true, or if the conclusion does not logically follow from the premises. This means a deductive argument must stand on valid, verifiable premises, and the conclusion is a logical result of the premises.

Straw Man Fallacy

The "straw man" fallacy consists of an oversimplification or distortion of opposing views. This fallacy is one of the most obvious and easily uncovered since it relies on gross distortions. The name comes from a side setting up a position so weak (the straw man) that is easily refuted.

Actor vs. dramatist

The dramatist must make sure that the venue for which he is writing will be physically able to handle the demands of his play. The dramatist must also be mindful of the audience for which he is writing as well as the abilities of the actors who will be portraying the characters he creates. The ability of the actor is crucial to the creation of a character because an actor can impose his or her own personality onto a character created by a dramatist. Some dramatists tend to write about characters in the abstract, creating characters from their imagination. Some dramatists create characters based on actual people. Ancient dramatists created characters for the actor who would play the role and both Shakespeare and Moliere's work was influenced by the actors for whom they were writing. The actor whom the dramatist has in mind when creating a character has a great impact on the creation of that character.

Deus ex machine

The term *deus ex machine* is Latin for "God out of a machine." The term originated in Greek tragedy where an actor playing the role of God was lowered onto the stage by some mechanical device. In modern usage, the term refers to a character or event that is suddenly introduced into a work of fiction in order to help resolve some problem or dilemma.

Practice Test

Practice Questions

Competency 001

1. Which form of drama, also known as creative drama, involves an instructor guiding participants to first imitate actual experiences and then reflect upon them?
    a. Product-centered drama
    b. Process-centered drama
    c. Natural-state drama
    d. Method acting

2. Theatre in Education, or TIE, is considered a mix of formal theatre and creative drama (also known as process-centered drama) where the outcome of a performance:
    a. Is undetermined and solely at the discretion of performers "in the moment."
    b. Is scripted, meaning actors are limited by specific dialog and movements.
    c. Has various versions that the performers must choose *before* performing.
    d. Is completely up to the teacher.

3. A high school drama class is studying the play *Huckleberry Finn.* The teacher asks two students to get in front of the class and act out the roles of Huck Finn and Tom Sawyer. However, she asks the students to rely on their imaginations and act as though Huck and Tom are 20 years older than they are in the actual play. This type of unscripted acting is called:
    a. Spontaneous depiction.
    b. Improvisation.
    c. In-depth characterization.
    d. Character relationship analysis.

4. If a drama teacher wanted to demonstrate pantomime to her students, she might do which of the following?
    a. Recite Edgar Allen Poe's "The Raven"
    b. Sing Evita's "Don't Cry for Me Argentina"
    c. Sit cross-legged in the center of the room and chant
    d. Attempt to tell a story using only facial expressions and bold gestures

5. A ninth-grade theatre class sits in a circle while their teacher lays a large rectangular piece of cloth in the center of the circle. Each student is asked to enter the circle, pick up the cloth, and answer the question: "What could this piece of fabric be?" The students are encouraged to use their imaginations while answering. This is an example of:
    a. A theatre game used as a warm-up.
    b. Ad-libbing to create a plot.
    c. A concentration exercise.
    d. Skill development to encourage group cohesion.

Use the information below to answer Question 6:

> You and your best friend are walking through a park and you find a diamond ring. You want to find the ring's rightful owner, but your friend insists on selling the ring for extra spending money.

6. A fourth-grade drama teacher instructs two of her students to act out the above scenario using improvisation. This exercise is intended to aid in the class's comprehension of which of the following components of drama?
   a. Conflict
   b. Climax
   c. Foreshadowing
   d. Role reversal

7. What is the most important difference between process-centered drama and production-centered drama?
   a. Production-centered drama always takes place on a main stage, while process-centered drama always takes place in a classroom.
   b. Process-centered drama is free, while production-centered drama has many financial costs involved.
   c. A teacher allows a high level of creative freedom in process-centered drama. In production-centered drama, there is a director and the outcome is structured and predetermined.
   d. Production-centered drama involves a high level of improvisation, whereas process-centered drama is entirely scripted.

8. Listening, reacting, engaging in eye contact, and thoroughly understanding prompts are all important elements when nurturing a student's ability to develop what broad skill?
   a. Effective interaction
   b. Performance
   c. Rehearsal
   d. Role playing

9. To encourage successful collaboration among members of an ensemble, a drama teacher must do all of the following except:
   a. Define performance goals.
   b. Involve all willing participants.
   c. Invite new ideas from the group.
   d. Force the group to make creative decisions without offering help.

10. There are two actors onstage discussing politics. Tim reflexively rolls his eyes after Barry makes a comment. Barry responds to Tim's eye roll by saying, "Okay, clearly we need to change the subject." Barry's response was due to:
   a. Vocal cues.
   b. Subtext.
   c. Script directions.
   d. Natural impulse.

11. Which of the following would be the most effective way for a director to create a sense of creative collaboration amongst his ensemble before the rehearsal process begins?
    a. He should take his cast members to a play so they can observe other actors before determining what type of actors they want to be.
    b. He should have a party so all cast members can get to know each other on a friendly basis.
    c. He should hold a table read-through of the script that involves every member of the ensemble, even those who have small parts.
    d. He should get cast members to do a simple warm-up that involves improvisation and theatre games.

12. Which of the following is the most important aspect of writing or choosing a script for a third-grade classroom?
    a. There needs to be a lesson learned at the end of the story.
    b. The script must be appropriate for both the performer(s) and the audience.
    c. The script must not call for expensive props.
    d. The dialogue must not contain offensive language.

13. Fill in the blank: When critiquing students' monologues, it is important to help them through the refining process by ____:
    a. Cutting content when their monologues are over five minutes in length.
    b. Rewriting and fine tuning verbiage so that all audience members can relate to the material.
    c. Encouraging them to stay in character for a full 24 hours to grasp the mood of the monologue.
    d. Making sure the student can identify with the character and is comfortable with the dialect and content.

Use the information below to answer Question 14:

A young girl walks along the beach with her dog as the waves tickle her feet. A boy approaches the girl and asks her if she would like to build a sandcastle with him.

14. You ask each student in your fifth-grade drama class to close their eyes while you read the above passage. Then, with their eyes opened, you ask each student to tell his or her own version of what happens next with the girl, the dog, and the boy on the beach. This is an example of using which source material?
    a. Memory
    b. Visualization
    c. Imagination
    d. Personal experiences

15. Fill in the blank: When reading or writing a script, character actions that occur while the character is speaking should appear in ____:
    a. Upper case.
    b. Bold font.
    c. Parentheses.
    d. Italics.

16. An important script element that appears in all capital letters and tells the reader about the current scene setting is known as what?
    a. Slug line
    b. Header
    c. Scene description
    d. Theme

17. With respect to actor placement onstage, the term "upstage" means what?
    a. The actor is toward the back of the stage, away from the audience.
    b. The actor is positioned at the front of the stage, close to the audience.
    c. The actor is exactly at the center of the stage.
    d. The actor is standing on an X on the stage that was put in place by the director.

18. A second-grade teacher divides half of her class into three groups and assigns a room (bathroom, kitchen, dining room, etc.) to each group. Each student picks an item or utensil that is vital to their assigned room. One student chooses a refrigerator, another chooses a mirror, another chooses a fork, etc. They are not allowed to say which item they chose aloud. The teacher picks a student and says, "I'm going to have a garage sale, and I'm going to put you up for sale." The student responds by saying, "No! You can't sell me." The student goes on to explain why the room he is standing in cannot function without him. If he picked a refrigerator, for example, he might say, "Your food would go rotten without me!" The other half of the class has to figure out which room the students are standing in based on their responses. This theatre game not only uses improvisation, but also teaches students:
    a. Critical thinking skills.
    b. Imagery.
    c. Prop placement.
    d. Collaboration.

19. Mood and setting can often be confused with one another. What is the main distinction between the two terms?
    a. Mood is created solely by the characters and their actions. Setting is the physical location of the play.
    b. Sensory details determine the mood, allowing the audience to feel certain emotions. Setting is what the audience sees in terms of set design.
    c. Mood is created by a lighting designer, while setting is created by a set designer.
    d. Setting is entirely dependent on the mood. They cannot exist without one another.

20. Fill in the blank: A common form of storytelling that involves manipulating inanimate objects to make them look like living beings is known as _____:
    a. Puppetry.
    b. Pantomime.
    c. Make-believe.
    d. Animation.

21. Finish the following sentence by selecting the best answer choice. Visiting your local library, joining theatre organizations, researching theatre topics online, and networking with fellow drama teachers are all ways to:
    a. Enhance social skills, which are extremely important for drama teachers.
    b. Utilize professional source materials.
    c. Increase your chances of getting a lead role in a community play.
    d. Complete a continuing education credit.

22. All of the following are examples of widely studied ancient theatre forms except:
    a. Greek.
    b. Roman.
    c. English Renaissance.
    d. Medieval.

23. Which of the following was a unique aspect of classical Greek theatre that set it apart from other genres?
    a. Actors never spoke on stage.
    b. Performances utilized just three actors.
    c. Greek theatres were very small, and could hold just 20 audience members at a time.
    d. Greek actors were the first to incorporate puppetry into performances.

24. What is *Commedia dell'Arte* and where did it originate?
    a. It is a physical, comical type of acting that broke through language barriers. It originated in Italy.
    b. It is slapstick humor that uses gestures instead of spoken words. It originated in Belgium.
    c. It is dark humor and sarcasm. It originated in America.
    d. It is pantomime that uses music to tell a story. It originated in Moscow.

25. The English Renaissance is a time period most known for its:
    a. Operas.
    b. Comedians.
    c. Playwrights.
    d. Classical musicians.

26. Method acting emerged in 20th century America with the help of Russian performer Constantin Stanislavski. All of the following are requirements of method acting except:
    a. Patience.
    b. Skilled listening.
    c. Astute focus.
    d. Sense of humor.

27. A seventh-grade drama teacher asks his students to close their eyes and think of their favorite cookies right out of the oven. He asks, "How does the smell of the cookies affect you?" The teacher then asks the students to perform an impromptu scene from grandma's house. Which technique did the drama teacher use?
    a. Sensory recall
    b. Focus
    c. Perception
    d. Characterization

28. According to Richard Boleslavsky, author of *Acting: The First Six Lessons,* a performer must hone certain skills to become successful. He stresses education of the body, education of the mind, and development of the soul. These are components of which type of acting?
    a. Practical aesthetics
    b. Meisner technique
    c. Method acting
    d. Active analysis

29. Analyzing each character in a script, studying biographical information, and understanding each characters' strengths and weaknesses are important aspects of:
    a. Developing character relationships.
    b. Script analysis.
    c. Plot development.
    d. Psychological dissection.

30. An eighth-grade theatre teacher asks her class to inhale by yawning, and then let out all the air by sighing as loudly as possible. This is an example of:
    a. Vocal projection.
    b. Pitch development.
    c. Vocal warm-up.
    d. Breath control.

31. A vocal teacher instructs his students to sing "Mary Had a Little Lamb" without consonants, stressing only the vowels. He asks his students to be aware of what shapes their mouths make during this exercise. This is an example of practicing:
    a. Diction.
    b. Tempo.
    c. Phrasing.
    d. Tone.

32. The forceful vocal projection that occurs when a performer uses her chest instead of her diaphragm while breathing will most likely result in:
    a. A lower pitch.
    b. Vocal injury.
    c. A higher pitch.
    d. Loss of vocal control.

33. Two commonly misused terms in theatre are pitch and tone. Choose the answer that best describes the difference between the two terms.
   a. Tone is the actual value of a note (B sharp, for example). Pitch is sound quality.
   b. There is no difference between the two terms. They are interchangeable.
   c. Pitch is the value of the note (C minor, for example). Tone measures the quality of the note's sound.
   d. Pitch is the value of a note sung by a performer. Tone is the value of a note played on a musical instrument.

34. Choose the answer that best finishes the following sentence. A neutral mask is ____:
   a. Without color.
   b. Made of organic materials.
   c. Without expression.
   d. Always flesh-colored.

35. If a drama teacher wanted to deepen his students' understanding of human emotions and characterization, he might bring which of the following to class?
   a. Costumes
   b. Commedia half-masks
   c. Comedy/tragedy masks
   d. Character masks

36. Charlie is playing the villain in his high school play. Before going onstage for his scene, he shakes his fist in the air to trigger the evil essence of his character. While he is onstage, his evil act starts to fade, so he envisions himself shaking his fist in order to recapture the nature of his character. This tactic is called:
   a. Psychological gesture.
   b. Character conceptualization.
   c. Mental movement.
   d. Chekhov method.

37. The director of a production has many duties. All of the following are assumed duties of a director except:
   a. Vocal coaching.
   b. Encouraging cohesion among cast mates.
   c. Interpreting and approving scripts.
   d. Collaborating with crew members.

38. A middle school theatre teacher finds a script that he is very passionate about for his seventh graders to perform. The only problem with the script is that it contains language that is inappropriate not only for his students, but also for the audience. Which of the following would be the best course of action for the teacher?
   a. Find a completely new script for the seventh graders.
   b. Omit the foul words from the script, but leave the plot line as is.
   c. Have the students rewrite the script in their own words.
   d. Leave the script as is so the original playwright won't be upset.

39. A director asks his entire company to form a circle, and then asks that cast members stand between crew members. Everyone is then directed to turn to their right so they are facing the back of the person standing next to them. On the director's count of three, everyone is to sit in the lap of the person behind them. If everyone does this correctly, the company will form a self-sustaining "chair circle." What is the director trying to create through this activity?
    a. A positive working environment for his cast and crew
    b. Distinction between crew members and actors
    c. Efficiency and productivity
    d. Competition between crew members and actors

40. A director is having a difficult time keeping his company members motivated during rehearsals. Rehearsals are four hours in length and will continue for another three weeks. Which of the following would be the most effective tactic to employ in this situation?
    a. The director should give the cast one week off from rehearsals.
    b. The director should collaborate with his cast to decide on a break time.
    c. The director should force the cast to have dinner together after rehearsals.
    d. The director should shorten rehearsals to two hours instead of four.

41. To ensure maximum dramatic effect, a director places actors onstage precisely where he wants them. What is this called?
    a. Positioning
    b. Staging
    c. Choreography
    d. Blocking

42. Drama teachers and directors often have to budget for theatrical performances. One main cost involved with putting on a production is purchasing scripts for cast members. It seems as though photocopying one script would be a logical way to cut costs. Why is photocopying scripts not a good idea?
    a. Photocopying scripts without the permission of the playwright is considered copyright infringement, and could result in an expensive lawsuit.
    b. Scripts are so inexpensive that it costs less to purchase them than to buy the paper and ink needed to photocopy them.
    c. Script pages can get lost or shuffled around during photocopying.
    d. It is better for cast members to share scripts in order to collaborate with fellow cast mates.

43. The character Hedy LaRue from *How to Succeed in Businesses Without Really Trying* is typically portrayed by a Caucasian woman. If a director wanted to cast an Asian American woman in his rendition of the play, what type of casting would this be?
    a. Adverse casting
    b. Diverse casting
    c. Nontraditional casting
    d. Curveball casting

44. When is a theatre production company required to pay royalty fees to a playwright for using his work?
    a. On opening night
    b. Every time admission is charged
    c. Any time the play is performed for an audience
    d. When the admission price exceeds five dollars per audience member

45. In order for a director to get an idea of a performer's capabilities and talent, he might ask the performer to read a script he or she has never seen before. This is called:
    a. Blind reading.
    b. Preliminary reading.
    c. Cite reading.
    d. Cold reading.

46. A theatre director hoping to produce a low-cost series of experimental skits would benefit from using which type of theatrical stage?
    a. Proscenium
    b. Black box
    c. Arena
    d. Thrust

47. What is the difference between a thrust stage and an arena?
    a. An audience can sit on three sides of a thrust stage; they can sit on all four sides of an arena.
    b. A thrust stage cannot utilize a backstage, whereas an arena can.
    c. An audience can only sit in front of a thrust stage; they can sit on three sides of an arena.
    d. A thrust stage can be an unused room or warehouse converted into a theatre; an arena is also known as a platform stage.

48. A director might hire a dramaturg for what purpose?
    a. To apply special effects makeup to the actors' faces and/or bodies
    b. To analyze dramatic text and research relevant historical facts in order to determine the artistic requirements of a specific production
    c. To incorporate lighting and sound effects to enhance the mood for the audience
    d. To aid in marketing efforts and increase ticket sales

49. What is theatre gel used for?
    a. It is a safety precaution in case someone gets burned by a stage light; theatre gel is applied to the skin to prevent scarring.
    b. Lighting technicians use theatre gels, or small transparent pieces of colored film, to change the mood with lighting.
    c. Sound technicians use theatre gels, or thick sound-resistant pads, to muffle sounds that are too loud.
    d. Costume designers use theatre gels, or adhesive liquids, to mend clothing when it tears or needs a quick hem.

50. You are backstage and you see an electrical cable with sparks flying out of it. According to most theatre safety rules and regulations, which of the following would be the most appropriate course of action?
    a. Get some electrical tape and wrap it around the area where sparks are present.
    b. Inform everyone on set and backstage so that a proper evacuation can take place.
    c. Call the fire department.
    d. Inform the stage manager or a lighting team member so they can assess the situation.

51. A document used by lighting designers and electricians that maps out exactly where each and every light bulb will be placed, which color will be used, and when they will be used is called what?
    a. Light map
    b. Lighting blue print
    c. Lighting key
    d. Light plot

52. A large instrument used for lighting that consists of a lamp socket and is surrounded by a reflector is called what?
    a. A specific light
    b. A general light
    c. A strip light
    d. A floodlight

53. When there are budget constraints, some directors and/or set designers will use a certain type of set that can be changed by merely adding one or two set pieces, which makes the set very versatile. What is this type of set called?
    a. Unit set
    b. Convertible set
    c. Multi set
    d. Uniform set

54. You were walking around barefoot backstage and cut your foot on an exposed nail. You find the first aid kit, clean the wound, and then put a bandage on your wound. What is the next course of action you should take?
    a. Take the first aid kit to the local pharmacy so you can properly restock it for others to use.
    b. Put the first aid kit in its designated area immediately in case someone else needs it.
    c. Give it to your stage manager so she can restock it.
    d. Report your injury to the stage manager.

55. As it relates to set design and scenery, a flat is:
    a. A set that resembles a European apartment.
    b. A portion of flat scenery, usually framed in wood and wrapped in canvas.
    c. A small piece of flat scenery hinged to another piece of flat scenery.
    d. A hinged metal plate used for suspending scenery.

56. Fill in the blank: A batten can best be described as _____:
    a. A long metal pole or pipe from which lighting, scenery, or curtains can be hung.
    b. A painted canvas or backcloth hung at the back of the stage.
    c. A hidden door in the stage where actors can enter and exit.
    d. A piece of cloth used to separate the stage from the audience.

57. Costumes can help deepen the audience's understanding of a character's social status, gender, occupation, and personality through clothing and accessories. Costumes can also do which of the following?
    a. Alter a performer's appearance
    b. Distinguish relationships among characters
    c. Convey changes in a character's age
    d. All of the above

58. A chart that lists characters that will be onstage, what they will be wearing, and possible wardrobe difficulties for every scene is called what?
    a. Costume plan
    b. Costume sketch
    c. Costume plot
    d. Costume script

59. How do most high schools obtain costumes for theatrical productions?
    a. High schools typically rent their costumes.
    b. A costume designer makes the costumes.
    c. Costumes are usually donated by students.
    d. Costumes can be rented, made, or donated.

60. If a makeup designer needed an actor to appear older than he actually is, which of the following would be the best makeup technique to use?
    a. After applying foundation to the face and neck, the makeup designer should highlight prominent facial muscles and darken the areas underneath the muscles.
    b. Before applying foundation to the face and neck, the makeup designer should highlight prominent facial muscles and darken the areas underneath the muscles.
    c. After applying foundation to the face and neck, the makeup designer should shade prominent facial muscles with dark tones and highlight the areas underneath the muscles.
    d. Before applying foundation to the face and neck, the makeup designer should shade prominent facial muscles with dark tones and highlight the areas underneath the muscles.

61. A makeup designer must have a thorough understanding of physiognomy. What is the definition of physiognomy?
    a. The practice of judging a person's character by studying his or her facial features
    b. The study of human facial features
    c. An understanding of facial euro-anatomy
    d. The practice of massaging one's face for relaxation purposes

62. According to most manufacturers of theatrical makeup, cosmetic products contain preservatives. What is the purpose of these preservatives?
    a. To prevent the transmission of infection due to makeup sharing
    b. To prolong the shelf life of the product
    c. To protect the product from color fading
    d. To prevent discoloration under theatrical lighting

63. Foam urethane and latex are standard materials used for making:
    a. Scenery backdrops
    b. Simple prosthetics
    c. Costume undergarments
    d. Non-slip pads for actors' shoes

64. You have just been hired by a local theatre to ensure rehearsals go smoothly. Your duties include recording blocking, prop, and lighting aspects, as well as making sure performers stay on script. What is your job title?
    a. Director
    b. Crew manager
    c. Technical director
    d. Stage manager

65. Backstage etiquette and safety are vital to a production's success. All of the following answer choices are examples of backstage safety precautions that should be taken by crew members except:
    a. Check all electrical cables and cords, making sure they are placed properly backstage so no one trips over them.
    b. Practice backstage procedures in light and dark conditions to become knowledgeable about set up and striking processes.
    c. Communicate with fellow crew members by using as few words as possible. Use code words if necessary to avoid lengthy conversations backstage.
    d. Practice striking in total darkness, which is important because the end of productions do not usually use lighting.

66. Set construction, sound mixing and recording, light hanging, and prop procurement are all aspects of:
    a. Process-centered theatre
    b. Practical theatre
    c. Technical theatre
    d. Artistic theatre

67. One type of theatre borrowed many cultural aspects from Medieval theatre, including plays with religious undertones that were performed in European churches and secular festivals. Which historical type of theatre was it?
    a. Renaissance
    b. Neoclassical
    c. Ancient Egyptian
    d. Indian

68. Of the following plays written by William Shakespeare, which one is considered a tragedy?
   a. As You Like It
   b. Macbeth
   c. Henry VIII
   d. A Lover's Complaint

69. Oscar Wilde (*The Importance of Being Earnest, Lady Windermere's Fan*) and George Bernard Shaw (*Pygmalion, Caesar and Cleopatra*) were both famous 19th century playwrights born in:
   a. Ireland.
   b. France.
   c. Russia.
   d. England.

70. Which genre of theatre pokes fun at current events and/or noteworthy people?
   a. Farce
   b. Comedy
   c. Satire
   d. Slapstick

71. A prime example of how live theatre has impacted society in the United States by creating jobs and attracting mass consumerism in a concentrated location is:
   a. Broadway.
   b. West End.
   c. Experimental theatre.
   d. Comedy clubs.

72. While most actors experience increases in confidence from performing in front of an audience, some individuals feel the negative emotional effects of theatre, which can include:
   a. Paranoia.
   b. Claustrophobia.
   c. Performance anxiety.
   d. Mood swings.

73. Which theatrical term best describes a dramatic outburst or a release of strong emotion by an actor or an audience member?
   a. Catharsis
   b. Alienation effect
   c. Performance purification
   d. Ablution

74. Bertolt Brecht was a famous playwright best known for coining a theatre technique that hinders an audience from relating too closely with characters so they can be observed from a more critical standpoint. What is this technique called?
   a. Audience breach
   b. Alienation effect
   c. Dissension effect
   d. Third-person effect

75. In order for someone writing a newspaper critique to give a theatre production a thorough evaluation, all of the following questions should be considered except:
    a. What is the financial impact of the production on the community?
    b. Did the lighting, set, and sound design help set the mood of the play?
    c. Why exactly did the director choose to produce this particular play?
    d. Which type of audience would most enjoy this production?

76. Publicity has a tremendous effect on how many people will view a particular production. Which of the following is the best way for a high school drama class to attract publicity for their play?
    a. Create posters to display around the school and the community
    b. Post the play's details (when, where, cost) on the school's website
    c. Write and send press releases to the local newspaper
    d. All of the above

77. What is the difference between a musical and an opera?
    a. A musical is sung in English; an opera is sung in Italian.
    b. Dance is typically incorporated in an opera; there is usually no dancing in musicals.
    c. An opera is usually sung all the way through (without dialogue); musicals contain spoken dialogue between songs.
    d. During an opera, a live orchestra fills the time between songs; during a musical, dance fills the time between songs.

78. What does TEKS stand for?
    a. Theatre Education, Knowledge, and Skills
    b. Texas Essential Knowledge and Skills
    c. Theatre Essentials and Knowledge of the Stage
    d. Texas Educators' Key to Success

79. Other than being categorized by grade level (K through 12), the Theatre TEKS is organized by four specific types of learning techniques. What are they?
    a. Perception, performance, relating history and culture to theatre, and response (also known as evaluation)
    b. Observation, memorization, interaction, and cooperation
    c. Critical thinking, role reversal, characterization, and peer review
    d. Cognition, research, creative interpretation, and assessment

80. In order to effectively educate students of diverse backgrounds, a drama teacher might do which of the following?
    a. Seek out plays and scripts written by minorities.
    b. Single out students of diverse backgrounds and make them do oral reports on their culture.
    c. None of the answers are appropriate. It is never a drama teacher's responsibility to educate students about diversity.
    d. Assign minority roles to Caucasian students.

81. As an eighth-grade drama teacher, you discover that Kim is drawn to costume design, Theo has a knack for sound mixing, and Robert enjoys set design. You ask each student to write an essay describing the aspect of theatre he or she would like to explore. What does this encourage?
   a. Self-evaluation
   b. Self-discovery
   c. Personal interpretation
   d. Conformism

82. Choose the best answer to complete the following sentence. A theatre teacher should always encourage creative expression in the classroom unless ____:
   a. It could be physically or emotionally harmful to students.
   b. A parent warns the teacher against it.
   c. It becomes motivational.
   d. It promotes collaboration among students.

83. Which method would be the most appropriate for teaching sixth-grade students how to critique others' performances?
   a. Conduct an open-ended conversation with anyone who wants to participate after a performance.
   b. After each act, encourage students to voice their opinions, good and bad.
   c. Instruct students to write down random thoughts about a performance while they are watching it.
   d. Before a performance, create a structured outline that includes the following headings: description, analysis, interpretation, and evaluation.

84. Choose the answer that best completes the following sentences. Process-centered drama is most appropriate for ____; product-centered drama is most appropriate for ____.
   a. Very young students who need to learn self expression; older students exploring a structured theatre environment.
   b. Older students exploring a structured theatre environment; very young students who need to learn self expression.
   c. Students who want to explore the artistic side of theatre; students who want to explore the technical side of theatre.
   d. Girls; boys.

85. Which situation would be an example of a junior high drama teacher using her knowledge of a student's prior experiences and interests to encourage participation and involvement in her classroom?
   a. She asks the quarterback of the football team to play the lead in the popular play about baseball, *Damn Yankees*.
   b. She asks the shiest girl in class to sing a song of her choosing in front of the class.
   c. She asks the star of the baseball team to recite the poem, "Casey at the Bat."
   d. She asks the class clown to play the very serious lead role in *The Crucible*.

86. Although every audience is different, it is important to teach students audience etiquette. All of the following are universally appropriate rules to follow when attending a performance except:
    a. Avoid speaking under all circumstances.
    b. Do not bring electronic gadgetry into a performance.
    c. Avoid falling asleep.
    d. Do not unwrap candy.

87. Choose the answer that best completes the following sentences. Two seventh-grade drama students are given the opportunity to portray characters of their choosing. Tonya chooses to portray her great-great-grandmother, while Carlos chooses to portray Malcolm X. Tonya's character portrayal is drawn from ____; Carlos's character portrayal is drawn from ____.
    a. History; current events
    b. Heritage; history
    c. Culture; diversity
    d. Personal experience; literature

88. Students in a high school drama class are told to partner up and create an original script that is based on the personal experiences of both partners. This activity is designed to promote what?
    a. A better understanding of interpersonal relationships
    b. Creative problem solving
    c. Self-confidence while performing in front of others
    d. Exploration of content-related material

89. A class of third-graders watches as an onstage performer stomps her feet when she doesn't get what she wants. The third-graders understand that the actress is expressing anger because they have grasped the concept of:
    a. Kinetics.
    b. Nonverbal communication.
    c. Gesturing.
    d. Body language.

90. Which of the following would not be considered a professional developmental resource for a high school drama teacher?
    a. Other theatre teachers
    b. Community theatre actors
    c. The World Wide Web
    d. A local art museum

Answers and Explanations

1. B: Process-centered drama is the correct answer because this method of teaching is focused on a child's ability to play and act out what they see in actual life. It is more perception based, whereas product-centered drama focuses on teaching acting skills. It is more structured. Method acting is when a performer uses his thoughts and emotions to convey a message to the audience. A child cannot fully understand product-centered drama or method acting until he understands process-centered drama. Natural-state drama does not exist.

2. A: Theatre in Education could be considered the stepping stone that lies between process-centered drama and product-centered drama. Like process-centered drama, it is unscripted. The student who is introduced to TIE, however, should have a working knowledge of performing in front of peers. The key focus of Theatre in Education is to teach performers how to be "in the moment." A teacher or instructor can give initial guidance, but the outcome is determined by the student.

3. B: Because neither student in the example is familiar with Huck Finn or Tom Sawyer as adults, they have to use their imaginations and prior knowledge of the characters to create a whole new scenario. Answer choices C and D can be eliminated because the situation does not call for character or relationship analysis. A term that describes on-the-spot performing would be a better answer choice. The situation calls for spontaneity, so answer choice A might look correct. However, a better term for this type of performance is *improvisation*.

4. D: Pantomime is conveying a message without using speech through the use of body movements, facial expressions, or gestures. This question can be answered by using the process of elimination. Answer choices A, B, and C are all instances where the drama teacher uses her voice as a teaching method. Answer choice D, though, indicates that the teacher is using only gestures and expressions to tell a story. D is the correct answer choice.

5. A: Games are vital when educating young children about the art of theatre. Theatre games that stimulate the imagination are most likely to be warm-up exercises. Plot creation and concentration, which are mentioned in answer choices B and C, would come after the initial warm-up. The exercise does relate to group cohesion, which is mentioned in answer choice D, but the focus of the game is not interaction. Therefore, D is incorrect.

6. A: The situation clearly shows two different viewpoints. This difference creates conflict between the two friends. If the scenario described a situation where the two friends were working toward a resolution, but the reader was still unaware of the consequences of their decision, answer choice B would be appropriate. Foreshadowing would have given hints as to where the story was headed, and role reversal is clearly not involved in this situation. Therefore, answer choices C and D are incorrect.

7. C: It is important to remember that process-centered drama involves an instructor encouraging his students to use their imaginations and reflect upon their own real-life experiences. Production-centered drama is much more structured, and relies on predetermined outcomes. Here is an easy way to distinguish process-centered drama from production-centered drama: The words "process" and "recess" end in the same three letters. If a child is learning *process*-centered drama, he or she is most likely to also have *recess* or playtime, as this method is learned during the lower grades. Production-centered drama can be thought of as a grand, main-stage production with more mature actors.

8. A: Learning how to effectively interact with others is extremely important to a child's understanding of theatre. In order to fully grasp effective interaction, one must develop certain skills, such as listening, reacting, engaging in meaningful eye contact, and taking note of prompts from other performers. Performance, rehearsal, and role playing are great methods for honing interaction skills, but a student must understand the basic fundamentals of effective interaction before they can perform these activities. .

9. D: In this question, look for the answer that does not belong. Answer choices A through C suggest that the teacher is providing encouragement, while answer choice D does not. A drama teacher should never be reluctant to assist an ensemble with group decisions. An instructor should always be helpful and offer suggestions when asked. Collaboration can be difficult in a theatre setting since there are multiple people supplying input. It is a teacher's duty to involve everyone, encourage new ideas, and define goals as a group.

10. B: According to the description of the situation, Tim *reflexively* rolled his eyes at Barry, meaning he did what came naturally in the moment. This gave the audience insight into his feelings without Tim having to come out and say it. There is no indication that he followed script directions or was prompted by a vocal cue, so neither answer choice A nor C is correct. Natural impulse is not always implied; it can be quite obvious. Therefore, answer D is not the best choice.

11. C: All of the answer choices in this question would effectively create a sense of creative collaboration among cast members. However, there is one answer choice that is better than the others. The most important thing to keep in mind when encouraging collaboration is to include everyone. That means the cast members with small roles should feel just as important as those with the lead roles. This will create positive cohesion throughout the entire rehearsal process. Answer C is the best choice since it involves all cast members and focuses on the play that will be performed.

12. B: Plenty of third-grade-level scripts *do* contain lessons at the end of the story. Typically, though, only fables are supposed to include a moral lesson. Therefore, answer choice A is incorrect. If a script called for expensive props or contained offensive language, it would not be suitable to be performed by third-graders or to be viewed by an audience. Therefore, while both answer choices C and D are correct, B is the better choice because it is broader and encompasses both C and d.

13. D: Performing a monologue can be unnerving for even the most experienced actor. When introducing young students to monologues, the most important thing to keep in mind is that they should feel comfortable with the content and dialect, and should be able to relate to the character in some way. Answer choices A through C are all good options when refining monologues, but establishing a comfort level between script and student is the most important aspect, making D the best choice.

14. C: The operative phrase in the question is *what happens next.* If the question called for a description, which would require students to use visualization skills, answer choice B would be the correct choice. The students most likely will use their memories and personal experiences as references in creating their stories, but because the teacher is asking *what's next,* the students have to use their imaginations more than anything else.

15. C: When formatting scripts, character names and headings appear in upper case letters. Therefore, choice A is incorrect. As a general rule, underlining is preferred over both bold and italic fonts, making answer choices B and D incorrect. Action while a character is speaking should be identified with parentheses. If a character is not speaking, action is simply listed without special formatting.

16. A: It is important to first recognize that "slug line" is another term for "scene heading." The term should not be confused with the term "header." The question is asking about a script element that appears in all capital letters and describes the current setting. The only two script elements that are written in all capital letters are character names and slug lines. Since the question does not reference character names, answer choice A is correct.

17. A: Here is an easy way to remember stage directions: There is an old wives' tale about stage construction that claims that stages used to be built on a slope (the back end was higher than the front). When a director wanted an actor to stand at the back of the stage, he literally meant, "Go *up* the stage." If the director wanted an actor positioned toward the front of the stage, he would say, "Go *down* the stage." Eventually, these directions were shortened to "upstage" and "downstage."

18. A: The children in this situation must apply critical thinking skills in order to successfully convey a message to the audience. They must *imagine* themselves in a specific room, *recall* which utensils or items belong in that room, and then take their thinking skills one step further by *deciding* why their item is necessary to the room. Answer choices B through D are not comprehensive enough to answer this question.

19. B: Mood relates to emotional responses. Audience members must use their senses to determine certain feelings, such as happiness, anger, sadness, and confusion. The director can evoke certain emotions through set design, costuming, and lighting choices. Setting can help determine mood. However, setting is concrete, as it is what the audience actually sees and hears. Mood is more abstract. Answer choice B best describes the difference between mood and setting.

20. A: Pantomime is an art form that uses gestures and bold facial expressions. It has nothing to do with manipulating objects to make them appear alive. Make-believe is often utilized in the art of puppetry, but it does not always require the use of inanimate objects. Animation occurs onscreen, not onstage, making choice D incorrect. Puppetry is the only art form that involves manipulating inanimate objects to make them look like living beings.

21. B: Professional source materials for both aspiring and practicing educators come in many forms. While visiting libraries, joining theatre organizations, researching, and networking *might* enhance social skills and increase the odds of being included in a community play, these activities do not involve the use of professional source materials. Neither answer choice A nor C is the *best* answer here. Continuing education credit is not covered in the TEKS, so answer choice D is incorrect.

22. C: The first form of theatre originated in ancient Greece. Some experts believe this happened as far back as 500 BC. The Romans developed their own form of theatre shortly after the decline of the Greek government, imitating many aspects of Greek theatre. Medieval theatre, which relied heavily on religious undertones, came next. There are other forms of ancient theatre, but Greek, Roman, and Medieval are the most commonly studied. The English Renaissance is too young to be considered "ancient," as it originated in the 16th century.

23. B: Classical Greek theatre used just three actors onstage, regardless of how many speaking roles there were. They simply went backstage and put on a mask to portray someone new. They did use their voices as powerful performing instruments, making choice A incorrect. Greek theatres were vast in size, accommodating many audience members. It is believed that Asians were the first to incorporate puppetry into theatre performances. Based on this information, answer choices C and D can be eliminated.

24. A: Translated from Italian, *Commedia dell'Arte* means "comedy of craft." It focused on the manner of the performance, not the subject or plot line of a story. Because the Italians were adapting skits from other European countries, they encountered language barriers. For that reason, they started using physical comedy and masks that displayed obvious emotions to reach broader audiences. Scripts were outlined, but not thoroughly written, as performers typically used improvisation to entertain their audience.

25. C: The English Renaissance is commonly known as "the age of Shakespeare." However, William Shakespeare was not the only famous playwright of this time period. Christopher Marlow, Francis Beaumont, Thomas Middleton, and countless other authors and playwrights emerged on the scene during the English Renaissance. There were also notable operas, comedies, and classical musicians, but this particular time period can *best* be distinguished by its playwrights.

26. D: This question is best approached by using the process of elimination and asking, "Which of the above answer choices does not belong?" It might also help to think of the word "method" and relate it to the term "methodical," which means organized. If someone is methodical, he is typically patient, has focus, and is a good listener. Therefore, answer choice D is the one that does not belong.

27. A: The teacher in the situation is asking his students to use their sense of smell to assist them during their impromptu performances. When a learning technique involves using

- 92 -

sight, smell, touch, hearing, or taste, chances are the teacher is stressing sensory recall. Focus and perception can both be used in the scenario, but neither answer choice is the *best* choice. Characterization really does not apply. Therefore, answer choices B through D are incorrect.

28. C: Practical aesthetics is related to scene breakdown and analysis. It is based on the teachings of Constantin Stanislavski, so answer choice A is incorrect. The Meisner technique was created by Sanford Meisner. It focuses on a series of all-inclusive exercises taught to improve improvisation, so answer choice B can be eliminated. Active analysis, also developed by Stanislavski, is an analytical technique that strengthens an actor's ability to solve problems and take action in the moment. Therefore, answer choice D can also be eliminated.

29. A: Analyzing and studying characters are important aspects of script analysis, but script analysis is much too broad to be the correct answer here. Plot development focuses on the storyline and occurs during the developmental stages before the script is complete. Psychological dissection is not a term that is used in theatre. The question is clearly asking for an answer that is related to better understanding a work's characters and their relationships with one another.

30. C: There are many types of vocal techniques in theater, including warm ups, strengthening exercises, and developmental exercises. It is important to distinguish them from each other. Vocal projection would not be the correct answer here because the teacher is asking her students to *yawn,* not necessarily use their full vocal capacity. Pitch development would require certain musical notes, and breath control would require increments of time. Therefore, answer choice C is the best answer.

31. A: Tempo is related to timing. It is not related to wording, so answer choice B is incorrect. Phrasing is more closely related to *which* words are sung, not *how* words are sung, so answer choice C is incorrect. Tone has nothing to do with vowels or mouth shape, just the quality of vocal sound, so answer choice D is incorrect. Diction is closely related to enunciation. Stressing vowels over consonants is a common vocal exercise used to improve clarity of vocal sound.

32. B: This question can be approached by using the process of elimination. If a performer uses her chest instead of her diaphragm while singing, a lower sound *may* occur, but it is unlikely. Therefore, answer choice A can be eliminated. A higher pitch and a loss of vocal control are both possible when breathing through the chest, but neither answer choice C nor D is the *best* answer. As an educator, it is important to stress *safety first* to students, so answer choice B is the best answer.

33. C: Here is an easy way to remember how to distinguish *pitch* from *tone* using word association. Think of a baseball pitcher. Now think of the *value* the pitcher brings to the team. The pitcher is so valuable that he is awarded Most Valuable Player of the year. *Pitch* is the *value* of a note. Now think of a quality control manager named Tony. Tony also plays the piano. *Tone* measures the *quality* of a note's sound.

34. C: It was Jacques Lecoq, an actor from Paris, who introduced neutral masks into the world of theatre. The term *neutral* has nothing to do with color or material. It simply means "without expression." Lecoq used neutral masks as an actor training tool to create a sense of

calm. He wanted his students to understand that while wearing the mask, they cannot be in the past or the future, just in the present. They must be fully aware of themselves and space.

35. D: In order for a student to understand human emotions and characterization, he must be able to recognize facial expressions. Character masks are full masks, each representing a different emotion, such as happy, sad, surprised, mad, etc. Costumes are typically not indicators of emotion, so answer choice A is incorrect. Commedia half-masks display *some* emotion, but their main purpose is to allow for the use of text, so answer choice B is not the best choice. Comedy/tragedy masks are limited in the expressions they can convey, only showing happiness and sadness. Therefore, answer choice D is not the best choice.

36. A: The psychological gesture was developed by the Russian actor and director Michael Chekhov in the early 20th century. His technique was one part physical (before going onstage) and one part visualization (while onstage). It was used when an actor needed to channel the essence of his character. Chekhov did not name the technique after himself, making answer choice D incorrect. Neither character conceptualization nor mental movement are methods related to theatre.

37. A: The operative word in the question is *assumed.* While a director of a production *might* lend a hand to a performer in need of vocal coaching, it is not one of his expected duties. Answer choice A is the one that does not belong. Encouraging cohesion among cast mates, interpreting and approving scripts, and collaborating with crew members are all regularly assumed duties that a successful director must perform.

38. B: According to the scenario in the question, the teacher is passionate about a particular script. Passion is extremely important and is closely connected to the success of a show. Therefore, finding a new script for the seventh graders is not the best option. Having the students rewrite the script might work, but would be a tedious process. Leaving the script "as is" is not an option since appropriateness is one of the most important aspects of script selection. Omitting the foul words is the best option.

39. A: By conducting a "chair circle," the director clearly wants to encourage relationships between cast and crew members that are friendly and comfortable. There is no indication that the director wants there to be competition or distinction between the two groups. If that was the case, he would have divided them into separate, opposing teams. Efficiency and productivity will *most likely* increase by conducting activities such as a "chair circle," but the main focus here is on positivity.

40. B: If a director was to give his cast a week off from rehearsals, they might start forgetting lines, or worse, become even more unmotivated. Therefore, answer choice A is not the best choice. Making cast members have dinner together might lower morale and hinder motivation if the cast feels forced, so answer choice C is not the best choice. To choose between answer choices B and C, select the *best* option. Shortening rehearsals may work, but collectively agreeing on break times promotes collaboration, which can be a powerful motivational device.

41. D: Director placement of an actor onstage could be considered *positioning,* but the technical theatre term is *blocking,* so answer choice A is incorrect. Staging is related to set design and prop placement, and has nothing to do with the placement of actors. Therefore,

answer choice B can be eliminated. Choreography is related to actor placement onstage, but only when specific dance movements are involved, making answer choice C incorrect.

42. A: The prices of scripts vary, so it cannot be assumed that purchasing scripts would be less expensive than photocopying them. Therefore, answer choice B can be eliminated. Script pages *can* get lost or shuffled during photocopying, but this is not a good enough reason on its own to purchase scripts *instead* of photocopying them, so answer choice C is incorrect. Sharing scripts is not a good idea because it is inconvenient. Therefore, answer choice D is incorrect.

43. C: Nontraditional casting is when a director gives a role to someone who does not "fit" a particular character description. This is not always related to diversity, and does not always involve giving a role to someone of one race when the character is typically played by someone of another race. For example, a director could give the role of Daddy Warbucks from the stage play *Annie* to a woman and change the character's name to Mama Warbucks. Adverse and curveball casting are not actual theatre terms.

44. C: A theatre is required to pay royalty fees to a playwright any time the play is performed in front of an audience. This includes dress rehearsals or trial runs that are conducted so actors can get a feel for performing in front of others. Often, spectators are not charged an admission. The question of when royalties should be paid has nothing to do with opening night or how much admission is charged, so answer choices A, B, and D are incorrect.

45. D: Blind reading is not used in the theatre industry, so answer choice A can be eliminated. While a cold read is indeed preliminary in nature, answer choice B is incorrect because the technical term is *cold.* Cite reading is when a performer runs through a piece of sheet music for the first time. It is not related to script reading, so answer choice C is incorrect.

46. B: Experimental theatre is often performed in what is called a black box theatre. This type of theatre can be a converted classroom, an abandoned warehouse, or even an old coffee shop. Usually, there are very few (if any) costs involved with holding performances in a black box theatre. Prosceniums, arenas, and thrusts would be more appropriate for productions that require structured and technical aspects, such as lighting and sound.

47. A: Simply put, a thrust can be described as something that is shoved or *thrust* into an audience from the back wall. Because a thrust is attached to the back wall, audience members can only sit on three sides of the stage. An arena, on the other hand, is typically positioned in the middle of a very large space. Audience members can see a performance from all four sides.

48. B: Answer choice A is incorrect because applying special effects makeup is the responsibility of a makeup designer. Answer choice C is incorrect because incorporating lighting is the responsibility of a lighting designer. Taking care of sound effects is the responsibility of a sound designer. Marketing and increasing ticket sales are the responsibilities of either a house manager or a marketing manager; so, answer choice D is also incorrect. A dramaturg is a person hired to analyze text and research historical facts relevant to a production.

49. B: Theatre gels, also known as *color gels*, are small pieces of film used to change lighting color. Gels have nothing to do with safety, nor are they in actual *gel* form, so answer choice A is incorrect. Sound technicians have no need for color gels, so answer choice C is incorrect. Costume designers would not have a need for color gels, so answer choice D is also incorrect.

50. D: No one other than trained professionals should attempt to fix an electrical cable, especially if sparks are present. Therefore, answer choice A is incorrect. Informing everyone about the potentially dangerous situation may cause panic. Therefore, answer choice B is incorrect. The stage manager or a lighting team member would most likely know how to fix the problem, so calling the fire department may not be necessary. Therefore, answer choice D is a better choice than answer choice c.

51. D: In order to correctly answer this question, one would have to be familiar with specific lighting terminology. Answer choices A through C are not terms that are used in the theatre industry. *Light plot*, though, is a commonly used term. It is a chart or document mapping out precise locations of lights and lighting fixtures. It also lists which color gels will be used and, most importantly, whether they will be used to illuminate, dim, or fade to black.

52. D: Specific lighting refers to a small, controlled area of light. Therefore, answer choice A is incorrect. General lighting involves a much vaster area than specific lighting. An entire stage can be illuminated with general lighting, and would obviously involve the use of more than one instrument. Therefore, answer choice B is incorrect. Strip lights are long troughs made of metal that are divided into components. Strip lights do not contain reflectors, so answer choice C is also incorrect.

53. A: A unit set is aptly titled because it consists of separate *units* that can easily be switched around to change the layout of a set. A unit set is *convertible* and can take on *multiple* shapes, but *unit set* is the technical theatre term. Therefore, answer choices B and C are incorrect. The term *uniform* indicates consistency, or something that is constant and not ever-changing. Therefore, answer choice D is incorrect.

54. B: It is vital to always have a first aid kit available to all members involved in a theatre production. Injuries can happen backstage, so a first aid kit should never leave its designated area. Taking it out of its designated area would be a bad idea because someone could injure themselves during the time when the first aid kit was removed. Therefore, answer choices A and C are incorrect. Reporting an injury should be done *after* the kit is returned to its designated area, so answer choice D would not be the next course of action in this situation.

55. B: A flat is a portion of a set, not a *type* of set. Therefore, answer choice A is incorrect. A small piece of scenery that is hinged to another piece of flat scenery is known as a *flipper*, so answer choice C is incorrect. A metal plate that is hinged and used for scenery suspension is called a *flying iron,* so answer choice D is incorrect. A flat is a piece of flat scenery that is framed in wood and usually wrapped in cloth or canvas.

56. A: A painted canvas or backcloth hung at the back of the stage is called a *backdrop*, so answer choice B is incorrect. A hidden door in the stage where actors can enter and exit is called a *trap*, so answer choice C is incorrect. A piece of cloth used to separate the stage from the audience is called a *curtain* or *grand drape*, so answer choice D is also incorrect.

57. D: Answer choice D is correct because costumes can have many functions onstage. Proper costuming can alter a performer's appearance, distinguish relationships among characters, and convey changes in a character's age *in addition to* deepening the audience's understanding of a character's social status, gender, occupation, and even personality. A costume designer has many important responsibilities. In many cases, he or she can enhance an audience member's experience.

58. C: Similar to a lighting plot, a costume plot is a chart or document created by the designer to inform her team of costuming directions. It lists each costume with accessories, which character will be wearing each costume, and when exactly they will appear onstage. While a costume plot is a *plan* that can be *sketched* or written out like a *script*, the technical term used by professionals in the industry is costume *plot*.

59. D: Theatre costumes can come from anywhere. There is no set standard with respect to how a high school should obtain costuming. Renting costumes can be more cost effective than hiring a seamstress or costume designer to make each wardrobe piece. Donated costumes are obviously even more cost effective than rented ones. Sometimes, when costumes are donated, a seamstress will add accessories to make an old costume or article of clothing more unique or more suitable for a specific performance.

60. A: Theatrical makeup application should start with foundation. All other techniques, such as shading, highlighting, color, and special effects, should go on *after* an even base of foundation is applied to clean skin. Answer choices B and D state that shading and highlighting should be applied before foundation, so both answer choices can be eliminated. Highlighting should be applied to the muscles, and shading should be applied underneath the muscles, so answer choice C is incorrect.

61. A: Physiognomy is the practice of judging a person's character by studying his or her facial features. It is important for a makeup designer to understand physiognomy because people associate character traits with certain facial features. For example, a makeup designer might add frown lines to an actor's face to portray a sad character. A makeup designer might also make an actor's mouth appear fuller than normal because audiences tend to view people with larger mouths as generous.

62. B: The preservatives in theatrical makeup are added to prolong the shelf life of the product. There are no other benefits of preservatives in makeup. They do not prevent the transmission of infection caused by sharing product. The only way to prevent infections is to refrain from sharing makeup. Preservatives will not prevent against color fading, nor will they prevent discoloration under bright theatre lights. Therefore, answer choices A, C, and D are all incorrect.

63. B: A simple prosthetic can be a scar, a wound, or a fake nose. Simple prosthetics are typically made from foam urethane and latex. Scenery backdrops might contain foam or other materials typically found in prosthetics, but answer choice B is not the best answer. Costume undergarments are typically made from cloth, so answer choice C is incorrect. Non-slip pads may be constructed out of latex, but answer choice D is not the *best* choice.

64. D: The director of a theatrical production oversees all artistic endeavors while maintaining astute focus on the performers. However, the director does not handle

- 97 -

recording duties. Therefore, answer choice A is incorrect. A crew manager leads backstage efforts, so answer choice B is incorrect. A technical director oversees lighting and sound plots, but would never follow a script to make sure an actor says the correct words. Therefore, answer choice C is not the *best* answer.

65. D: Checking all electrical cables and cord placement so that no one trips over them, practicing backstage procedures in light and dark conditions to familiarize oneself with set up and striking processes, and communicating with other crew members in as few words as possible are all important aspects of backstage etiquette and safety. Striking a set in total darkness, however, is never a good idea. Crew members should always have a flashlight handy.

66. C: Process-centered *drama*, not *theatre,* is a learning technique, not a type of production. Therefore, answer choice A is incorrect. Practical theatre is a term rarely used in the theatre industry today, so answer choice B can be eliminated. Artistic theatre focuses on the actors and the dramatic performance, whereas technical theatre focuses on set construction, sound mixing and recording, light hanging, prop procurement, and all other aspects of theatre that are undetected by the audience.

67. A: Neoclassical theatre was not known for performances with religious undertones. Rather, it was known for its grandiosity, ornate costumes, and melodrama. Therefore, answer choice B is incorrect. Ancient Egyptian theatre did contain religious undertones, but it did not borrow cultural aspects from Medieval theatre, so answer choice C is not the best choice. Indian theatre focused more on rituals and depictions of everyday life, so answer choice D is incorrect.

68. B: *As You Like It* is a comedy by William Shakespeare, so answer choice A is incorrect. *Henry VIII* is considered a historical play, so answer choice C is incorrect. Shakespeare wrote *A Lover's Complaint* as a poem, so answer choice D is also incorrect. Of the answer choices, *Macbeth* is the only Shakespearian play that is considered a tragedy.

69. A: While it would be impossible to memorize every playwright, their works, and where they were from, it is important to memorize a few of the greats. Despite spending a good portion of their writing careers in England, Oscar Wilde and George Bernard Shaw were both born in Ireland. John Millington Synge (*The Playboy of the Western World*) had his plays performed in the famous Abbey Theatre in Dublin, Ireland. Edmond Rostand (*Cyrano de Bergerac*) hailed from France. Anton Chekhov (*The Marriage Proposal* and *The Three Sisters*) was from Russia.

70. C: A farce can be recognized by its outlandish, physical nature. Plots are fast-paced and typically involve improbable circumstances, so answer choice A is incorrect. The term *comedy* is too broad to be the *best* choice here, so answer choice B is incorrect. Slapstick can be identified by exaggerated, sometimes violent gestures, so answer choice D is incorrect. Satire is the only genre that regularly pokes fun at famous people and/or current events.

71. A: Broadway has impacted society by bringing countless jobs and mass consumerism to the United States, specifically New York. The West End has done the same thing. The West End, however, is in London, England. Therefore, answer choice B is incorrect. Experimental theatre has done little in terms of job creation and mass consumerism, mainly because it appeals to audiences and producers on a budget. Therefore, answer choice C is incorrect. Comedy clubs have created some jobs and generated some consumerism, but their impact is small compared to Broadway. Therefore, answer choice D is not the best choice.

72. C: Paranoia can be related to anxiety, but is more closely linked with delusion, which is rarely associated with performing. Therefore, answer choice A is incorrect. Claustrophobia is a fear of tight spaces, and has nothing to do with performance, making answer choice B incorrect. Mood swings can be associated with actors, as actors tend to be dramatic not only onstage, but also in real life. Performance anxiety, however, would be the *best* answer choice for this particular question.

73. A: As it relates to theatre, catharsis is a term that means "to purge the emotions." The terms *purification* and *ablution* have similar connotations, meaning "to cleanse or purify," but neither term is commonly used in the theatre industry. Therefore, answer choices C and D are incorrect. The alienation effect is when a director wants to distance the audience from the characters so they can be observed and critiqued from a non-emotional standpoint. Therefore, answer choice B is incorrect.

74. B: In order to approach this question, one must be able to identify commonly used theatre terms. The only actual theatre term in the answer choices is *alienation effect*. Neither *audience breach* nor *dissection effect* are actual techniques. Someone unfamiliar with theatre terminology, however, may choose one of these answers based on context clues. The third-person effect does exist, but does not relate to the theatre industry. Therefore, answer choices A, C, and D can all be eliminated.

75. A: A good theatre critic adheres to certain guidelines when evaluating productions. These guidelines can typically be categorized under who, what, why, and how. A critic would discuss who acted in the play, what emotions he felt, why the director chose that particular play, and how the technical aspects enhanced the overall feel of the play. The financial impact of a production on a community does not fall under the guidelines commonly followed by theatre critics.

76. D: Because high schools usually do not have the funding available to hire marketers or advertising firm, students and teachers must be creative. Making posters to display around the school and the community, posting the play's details on the school's website, and sending press releases to the local newspaper are all wonderful ways to promote a production for little to no cost. Therefore, answer choice D is correct.

77. C: Operas and musicals can be sung or performed in any language, so answer choice A is incorrect. There is typically no dancing in operas, whereas there is almost always dancing in musicals, so answer choice B is incorrect. The time between songs can be filled with an orchestra *and* dancing in musicals, so answer choice D is incorrect. The main difference is that operas are usually sung all the way through, while musicals contain spoken dialogue between songs.

78. B: TEKS does not stand for Texas Essential Knowledge and Skills, Theatre Essentials and Knowledge of the Stage, or Texas Educators' Key to Success. Therefore, answer choices A, C, and D can be eliminated. Not only is it important to know that TEKS stands for Texas Essential Knowledge and Skills, but it is also vital to understand that it is the official curriculum of the state of Texas.

79. A: In order to approach this question, one should look at each word in the answer choices. In answer choice B, the term *interaction* is too closely related to *cooperation*.

Therefore, answer choice B is not the best choice. Role-reversal is an acting technique, not a learning technique, so answer choice C can be eliminated. Finally, none of the items listed in answer choice D stress the importance of relating history and culture, which is one of the most important learning techniques according to the Theatre TEKS. Therefore, answer choice D can be eliminated.

80. A: To effectively stress diversity in the classroom, a teacher should introduce scripts containing multicultural themes and characters of all ethnic backgrounds. It would never be a good idea to single out a student of a different race or cultural heritage for any reason, so answer choice B is incorrect. Teaching diversity is indeed part of the TEKS curriculum, so answer choice C is incorrect. Assigning minority roles to Caucasian students would be more closely related to nontraditional casting, not diversity in education, so answer choice D is incorrect.

81. B: A teacher must be able to recognize certain traits and abilities in each student in order to guide them toward a successful life path. Self-evaluation would come *after* self-discovery, so answer choice A is not the best choice. To encourage self-discovery is to foster individuality, which is the opposite of conformism, so answer choice D is incorrect. Personal interpretation would call for creativity, not exploration, so answer choice C is incorrect.

82. A: A teacher must encourage creative expression in students, but even more vital is ensuring the physical and mental safety of students. While it is a good idea to take parental warnings into consideration, answer choice B is not the *best* choice. There would be no need to hinder creativity if it became a motivational force for a student, so answer choice C can be eliminated. There would also be no need to thwart creativity if it promoted collaboration among students, so answer choice D is incorrect.

83. D: Conducting open-ended conversations to critique a performance can be a drawn out and unorganized process, especially if students are new to critiquing. Therefore, answer choice A is incorrect. Asking for opinions or instructing students to write down random thoughts would be chaotic approaches to critiquing, so answer choices B and C are not the best choices. Younger students should be introduced to a structured outline that allows them to describe, analyze, interpret, and evaluate others' performances.

84. A: Process-centered drama is most appropriate for very young students who need to learn self-expression, whereas product-centered drama is most appropriate for older students exploring a structured theatre environment. Therefore, answer choice B is incorrect. Students who want to explore the artistic and technical aspects of theatre would likely be too mature for process-centered drama. Therefore, answer choice C is not the best choice. Drama at the K through 12 levels should not be gender specific, so answer choice D is incorrect.

85. C: The operative phrase in the question is *prior experience*. Answer choice A gives no indication that the football player has prior baseball experience, so answer choice A is incorrect. If a student is known for being shy, and not necessarily her singing skills, she is unlikely to feel comfortable singing in front of the class. Therefore, answer choice B is incorrect. Given his prior experience with comedy, a class clown would be more likely to take on a comedic role than a serious role. Therefore, answer choice D is incorrect.

86. A: Bringing electronic gadgetry into a performance, falling asleep, and unwrapping candy with noisy wrappers should be avoided when watching a theatre performance. It is very important to stress these rules of etiquette to students so they will be able to show respect for the actors onstage. If a student did not hear something, it is perfectly acceptable to quietly ask a neighbor for clarification. There are also times when performers interact with audience members, so speaking back would be necessary.

87. B: If Tonya's great-great-grandmother was a historical figure, her portrayal would be based on history *and* heritage. However, Carlos's portrayal of Malcolm X is not based on a current event, so answer choice A is incorrect. There is no indication that Tonya's great-great-grandmother came from a different culture, so answer choice C is not the best choice. Personal experience is typically not relevant during portrayals since portrayals are based on someone else. Therefore, answer choice D is incorrect.

88. A: Partnering students is a great way to promote a better understanding of interpersonal relationships. While problems may arise that need creative problem solving, that is not the focus of the activity, so answer choice B is not the *best* choice. A student may become more confident after being partnered up with another student, but the focus of the activity is on understanding partnerships and relationship building, so answer choice C is incorrect. Exploration of content-related material is not relevant in the scenario, so answer choice D is incorrect.

89. B: By stomping her feet, the actress in the question is communicating her feelings of anger to the audience without using words. Kinetics and gesturing refer to actual body movements, but don't necessarily have to have an emotion attached. Therefore, answer choices A and C are incorrect. Body language relates to positioning and how an individual is feeling internally as opposed to what the person wants to externally communicate to others, so answer choice D is not the best choice.

90. D: There are many professional development resources available to high school teachers today. One of the best resources to tap into would be other theatre teachers, whether they are in the same school or in another part of the country. Theatre teachers should familiarize themselves with local community actors and conduct research online. An art museum might inspire a lesson plan, but it would be a better professional resource for an art teacher. Therefore, answer choice D is the one that does not belong.

Secret Key #1 - Time is Your Greatest Enemy

Pace Yourself

Wear a watch. At the beginning of the test, check the time (or start a chronometer on your watch to count the minutes), and check the time after every few questions to make sure you are "on schedule."

If you are forced to speed up, do it efficiently. Usually one or more answer choices can be eliminated without too much difficulty. Above all, don't panic. Don't speed up and just begin guessing at random choices. By pacing yourself, and continually monitoring your progress against your watch, you will always know exactly how far ahead or behind you are with your available time. If you find that you are one minute behind on the test, don't skip one question without spending any time on it, just to catch back up. Take 15 fewer seconds on the next four questions, and after four questions you'll have caught back up. Once you catch back up, you can continue working each problem at your normal pace.

Furthermore, don't dwell on the problems that you were rushed on. If a problem was taking up too much time and you made a hurried guess, it must be difficult. The difficult questions are the ones you are most likely to miss anyway, so it isn't a big loss. It is better to end with more time than you need than to run out of time.

Lastly, sometimes it is beneficial to slow down if you are constantly getting ahead of time. You are always more likely to catch a careless mistake by working more slowly than quickly, and among very high-scoring test takers (those who are likely to have lots of time left over), careless errors affect the score more than mastery of material.

Secret Key #2 - Guessing is not Guesswork

You probably know that guessing is a good idea - unlike other standardized tests, there is no penalty for getting a wrong answer. Even if you have no idea about a question, you still have a 20-25% chance of getting it right.

Most test takers do not understand the impact that proper guessing can have on their score. Unless you score extremely high, guessing will significantly contribute to your final score.

Monkeys Take the Test

What most test takers don't realize is that to insure that 20-25% chance, you have to guess randomly. If you put 20 monkeys in a room to take this test, assuming they answered once per question and behaved themselves, on average they would get 20-25% of the questions correct. Put 20 test takers in the room, and the average will be much lower among guessed questions. Why?

1. The test writers intentionally write deceptive answer choices that "look" right. A test taker has no idea about a question, so picks the "best looking" answer, which is often wrong. The monkey has no idea what looks good and what doesn't, so will consistently be lucky about 20-25% of the time.
2. Test takers will eliminate answer choices from the guessing pool based on a hunch or intuition. Simple but correct answers often get excluded, leaving a 0% chance of being correct. The monkey has no clue, and often gets lucky with the best choice.

This is why the process of elimination endorsed by most test courses is flawed and detrimental to your performance- test takers don't guess, they make an ignorant stab in the dark that is usually worse than random.

$5 Challenge

Let me introduce one of the most valuable ideas of this course- the $5 challenge:

You only mark your "best guess" if you are willing to bet $5 on it.
You only eliminate choices from guessing if you are willing to bet $5 on it.

Why $5? Five dollars is an amount of money that is small yet not insignificant, and can really add up fast (20 questions could cost you $100). Likewise, each answer choice on one question of the test will have a small impact on your overall score, but it can really add up to a lot of points in the end.

The process of elimination IS valuable. The following shows your chance of guessing it right:

If you eliminate wrong answer choices until only this many remain:	Chance of getting it correct:

However, if you accidentally eliminate the right answer or go on a hunch for an incorrect answer, your chances drop dramatically: to 0%. By guessing among all the answer choices, you are GUARANTEED to have a shot at the right answer.

1	100%
2	50%
3	33%

That's why the $5 test is so valuable- if you give up the advantage and safety of a pure guess - it had better be worth the risk.

What we still haven't covered is how to be sure that whatever guess you make is truly random. Here's the easiest way:

Always pick the first answer choice among those remaining.

Such a technique means that you have decided, **before you see a single test question**, exactly how you are going to guess- and since the order of choices tells you nothing about which one is correct, this guessing technique is perfectly random.

This section is not meant to scare you away from making educated guesses or eliminating choices- you just need to define when a choice is worth eliminating. The $5 test, along with a pre-defined random guessing strategy, is the best way to make sure you reap all of the benefits of guessing.

Secret Key #3 - Practice Smarter, Not Harder

Many test takers delay the test preparation process because they dread the awful amounts of practice time they think necessary to succeed on the test. We have refined an effective method that will take you only a fraction of the time.

There are a number of "obstacles" in your way to succeed. Among these are answering questions, finishing in time, and mastering test-taking strategies. All must be executed on the day of the test at peak performance, or your score will suffer. The test is a mental marathon that has a large impact on your future.

Just like a marathon runner, it is important to work your way up to the full challenge. So first you just worry about questions, and then time, and finally strategy:

Success Strategy

1. Find a good source for practice tests.
2. If you are willing to make a larger time investment, consider using more than one study guide- often the different approaches of multiple authors will help you "get" difficult concepts.
3. Take a practice test with no time constraints, with all study helps "open book." Take your time with questions and focus on applying strategies.
4. Take a practice test with time constraints, with all guides "open book."
5. Take a final practice test with no open material and time limits

If you have time to take more practice tests, just repeat step 5. By gradually exposing yourself to the full rigors of the test environment, you will condition your mind to the stress of test day and maximize your success.

Secret Key #4 - Prepare, Don't Procrastinate

Let me state an obvious fact: if you take the test three times, you will get three different scores. This is due to the way you feel on test day, the level of preparedness you have, and, despite the test writers' claims to the contrary, some tests WILL be easier for you than others.

Since your future depends so much on your score, you should maximize your chances of success. In order to maximize the likelihood of success, you've got to prepare in advance. This means taking practice tests and spending time learning the information and test taking strategies you will need to succeed.

Never take the test as a "practice" test, expecting that you can just take it again if you need to. Feel free to take sample tests on your own, but when you go to take the official test, be prepared, be focused, and do your best the first time!

Secret Key #5 - Test Yourself

Everyone knows that time is money. There is no need to spend too much of your time or too little of your time preparing for the test. You should only spend as much of your precious time preparing as is necessary for you to get the score you need.

Once you have taken a practice test under real conditions of time constraints, then you will know if you are ready for the test or not.

If you have scored extremely high the first time that you take the practice test, then there is not much point in spending countless hours studying. You are already there.

Benchmark your abilities by retaking practice tests and seeing how much you have improved. Once you score high enough to guarantee success, then you are ready.

If you have scored well below where you need, then knuckle down and begin studying in earnest. Check your improvement regularly through the use of practice tests under real conditions. Above all, don't worry, panic, or give up. The key is perseverance!

Then, when you go to take the test, remain confident and remember how well you did on the practice tests. If you can score high enough on a practice test, then you can do the same on the real thing.

General Strategies

The most important thing you can do is to ignore your fears and jump into the test immediately- do not be overwhelmed by any strange-sounding terms. You have to jump into the test like jumping into a pool- all at once is the easiest way.

Make Predictions

As you read and understand the question, try to guess what the answer will be. Remember that several of the answer choices are wrong, and once you begin reading them, your mind will immediately become cluttered with answer choices designed to throw you off. Your mind is typically the most focused immediately after you have read the question and digested its contents. If you can, try to predict what the correct answer will be. You may be surprised at what you can predict.

Quickly scan the choices and see if your prediction is in the listed answer choices. If it is, then you can be quite confident that you have the right answer. It still won't hurt to check the other answer choices, but most of the time, you've got it!

Answer the Question

It may seem obvious to only pick answer choices that answer the question, but the test writers can create some excellent answer choices that are wrong. Don't pick an answer just because it sounds right, or you believe it to be true. It MUST answer the question. Once you've made your selection, always go back and check it against the question and make sure that you didn't misread the question, and the answer choice does answer the question posed.

Benchmark

After you read the first answer choice, decide if you think it sounds correct or not. If it doesn't, move on to the next answer choice. If it does, mentally mark that answer choice. This doesn't mean that you've definitely selected it as your answer choice, it just means that it's the best you've seen thus far. Go ahead and read the next choice. If the next choice is worse than the one you've already selected, keep going to the next answer choice. If the next choice is better than the choice you've already selected, mentally mark the new answer choice as your best guess.

The first answer choice that you select becomes your standard. Every other answer choice must be benchmarked against that standard. That choice is correct until proven otherwise by another answer choice beating it out. Once you've decided that no other answer choice seems as good, do one final check to ensure that your answer choice answers the question posed.

Valid Information

Don't discount any of the information provided in the question. Every piece of information may be necessary to determine the correct answer. None of the information in the question is there to throw you off (while the answer choices will certainly have information to throw you off). If two seemingly unrelated topics are discussed, don't ignore either. You can be confident there is a relationship, or it wouldn't be included in the question, and you are probably going to have to determine what that relationship is to find the answer.

Avoid "Fact Traps"

Don't get distracted by a choice that is factually true. Your search is for the answer that answers the question. Stay focused and don't fall for an answer that is true but incorrect. Always go back to the question and make sure you're choosing an answer that actually answers the question and is not just a true statement. An answer can be factually correct, but it MUST answer the question asked. Additionally, two answers can both be seemingly correct, so be sure to read all of the answer choices, and make sure that you get the one that BEST answers the question.

Milk the Question

Some of the questions may throw you completely off. They might deal with a subject you have not been exposed to, or one that you haven't reviewed in years. While your lack of knowledge about the subject will be a hindrance, the question itself can give you many clues that will help you find the correct answer. Read the question carefully and look for clues. Watch particularly for adjectives and nouns describing difficult terms or words that you don't recognize. Regardless of if you completely understand a word or not, replacing it with a synonym either provided or one you more familiar with may help you to understand what the questions are asking. Rather than wracking your mind about specific detailed information concerning a difficult term or word, try to use mental substitutes that are easier to understand.

The Trap of Familiarity

Don't just choose a word because you recognize it. On difficult questions, you may not recognize a number of words in the answer choices. The test writers don't put "make-believe" words on the test; so don't think that just because you only recognize all the words in one answer choice means that answer choice must be correct. If you only recognize words in one answer choice, then focus on that one. Is it correct? Try your best to determine if it is correct. If it is, that is great, but if it doesn't, eliminate it. Each word and answer choice you eliminate increases your chances of getting the question correct, even if you then have to guess among the unfamiliar choices.

Eliminate Answers

Eliminate choices as soon as you realize they are wrong. But be careful! Make sure you consider all of the possible answer choices. Just because one appears right, doesn't mean that the next one won't be even better! The test writers will usually put more than one good answer choice for every question, so read all of them. Don't worry if you are stuck between two that seem right. By getting down to just two remaining possible choices, your odds are now 50/50. Rather than wasting too much time, play the odds. You are guessing, but guessing wisely, because you've been able to knock out some of the answer choices that you know are wrong. If you are eliminating choices and realize that the last answer choice you are left with is also obviously wrong, don't panic. Start over and consider each choice again. There may easily be something that you missed the first time and will realize on the second pass.

Tough Questions

If you are stumped on a problem or it appears too hard or too difficult, don't waste time. Move on! Remember though, if you can quickly check for obviously incorrect answer choices, your chances of guessing correctly are greatly improved. Before you completely give up, at least try to knock out a couple of possible answers. Eliminate what you can and then guess at the remaining answer choices before moving on.

Brainstorm

If you get stuck on a difficult question, spend a few seconds quickly brainstorming. Run through the complete list of possible answer choices. Look at each choice and ask yourself, "Could this answer the question satisfactorily?" Go through each answer choice and consider it independently of the other. By systematically going through all possibilities, you may find something that you would otherwise overlook. Remember that when you get stuck, it's important to try to keep moving.

Read Carefully

Understand the problem. Read the question and answer choices carefully. Don't miss the question because you misread the terms. You have plenty of time to read each question thoroughly and make sure you understand what is being asked. Yet a happy medium must be attained, so don't waste too much time. You must read carefully, but efficiently.

Face Value

When in doubt, use common sense. Always accept the situation in the problem at face value. Don't read too much into it. These problems will not require you to make huge leaps of logic. The test writers aren't trying to throw you off with a cheap trick. If you have to go beyond creativity and make a leap of logic in order to have an answer choice answer the question, then you should look at the other answer choices. Don't overcomplicate the problem by creating theoretical relationships or explanations that will warp time or space. These are normal problems rooted in reality. It's just that the applicable relationship or explanation may not be readily apparent and you have to figure things out. Use your common sense to interpret anything that isn't clear.

Prefixes

If you're having trouble with a word in the question or answer choices, try dissecting it. Take advantage of every clue that the word might include. Prefixes and suffixes can be a huge help. Usually they allow you to determine a basic meaning. Pre- means before, post- means after, pro - is positive, de- is negative. From these prefixes and suffixes, you can get an idea of the general meaning of the word and try to put it into context. Beware though of any traps. Just because con is the opposite of pro, doesn't necessarily mean congress is the opposite of progress!

Hedge Phrases

Watch out for critical "hedge" phrases, such as likely, may, can, will often, sometimes, often, almost, mostly, usually, generally, rarely, sometimes. Question writers insert these hedge phrases to cover every possibility. Often an answer choice will be wrong simply because it leaves no room for exception. Avoid answer choices that have definitive words like "exactly," and "always".

Switchback Words

Stay alert for "switchbacks". These are the words and phrases frequently used to alert you to shifts in thought. The most common switchback word is "but". Others include although, however, nevertheless, on the other hand, even though, while, in spite of, despite, regardless of.

New Information

Correct answer choices will rarely have completely new information included. Answer choices typically are straightforward reflections of the material asked about and will directly relate to the question. If a new piece of information is included in an answer choice that doesn't even seem to relate to the topic being asked about, then that answer choice is likely incorrect. All of the information needed to answer the question is usually provided for you, and so you should not have to make guesses that are unsupported or choose answer choices that require unknown information that cannot be reasoned on its own.

Time Management

On technical questions, don't get lost on the technical terms. Don't spend too much time on any one question. If you don't know what a term means, then since you don't have a dictionary, odds are you aren't going to get much further. You should immediately recognize terms as whether or not you know them. If you don't, work with the other clues that you have, the other answer choices and terms provided, but don't waste too much time trying to figure out a difficult term.

Contextual Clues

Look for contextual clues. An answer can be right but not correct. The contextual clues will help you find the answer that is most right and is correct. Understand the context in which a phrase or statement is made. This will help you make important distinctions.

Don't Panic

Panicking will not answer any questions for you. Therefore, it isn't helpful. When you first see the question, if your mind goes blank, take a deep breath. Force yourself to mechanically go through the steps of solving the problem and using the strategies you've learned.

Pace Yourself

Don't get clock fever. It's easy to be overwhelmed when you're looking at a page full of questions, your mind is full of random thoughts and feeling confused, and the clock is ticking down faster than you would like. Calm down and maintain the pace that you have set for yourself. As long as you are on track by monitoring your pace, you are guaranteed to have enough time for yourself. When you get to the last few minutes of the test, it may seem like you won't have enough time left, but if you only have as many questions as you should have left at that point, then you're right on track!

Answer Selection

The best way to pick an answer choice is to eliminate all of those that are wrong, until only one is left and confirm that is the correct answer. Sometimes though, an answer choice may immediately look right. Be careful! Take a second to make sure that the other choices are not equally obvious. Don't make a hasty mistake. There are only two times that you should stop before checking other answers. First is when you are positive that the answer choice you have selected is correct. Second is when time is almost out and you have to make a quick guess!

Check Your Work

Since you will probably not know every term listed and the answer to every question, it is important that you get credit for the ones that you do know. Don't miss any questions through careless mistakes. If at all possible, try to take a second to look back over your answer selection and make sure you've selected the correct answer choice and haven't made a costly careless mistake (such as marking an answer choice that you didn't mean to mark). This quick double check should more than pay for itself in caught mistakes for the time it costs.

Beware of Directly Quoted Answers

Sometimes an answer choice will repeat word for word a portion of the question or reference section. However, beware of such exact duplication – it may be a trap! More than likely, the correct choice will paraphrase or summarize a point, rather than being exactly the same wording.

Slang

Scientific sounding answers are better than slang ones. An answer choice that begins "To compare the outcomes…" is much more likely to be correct than one that begins "Because some people insisted…"

Extreme Statements

Avoid wild answers that throw out highly controversial ideas that are proclaimed as established fact. An answer choice that states the "process should be used in certain situations, if…" is much more likely to be correct than one that states the "process should be discontinued completely." The first is a calm rational statement and doesn't even make a definitive, uncompromising stance, using a hedge word "if" to provide wiggle room, whereas the second choice is a radical idea and far more extreme.

Answer Choice Families

When you have two or more answer choices that are direct opposites or parallels, one of them is usually the correct answer. For instance, if one answer choice states "x increases" and another answer choice states "x decreases" or "y increases," then those two or three answer choices are very similar in construction and fall into the same family of answer choices. A family of answer choices is when two or three answer choices are very similar in construction, and yet often have a directly opposite meaning. Usually the correct answer choice will be in that family of answer choices. The "odd man out" or answer choice that doesn't seem to fit the parallel construction of the other answer choices is more likely to be incorrect.

Special Report: What Your Test Score Will Tell You About Your IQ

Did you know that most standardized tests correlate very strongly with IQ? In fact, your general intelligence is a better predictor of your success than any other factor, and most tests intentionally measure this trait to some degree to ensure that those selected by the test are truly qualified for the test's purposes.

Before we can delve into the relation between your test score and IQ, I will first have to explain what exactly is IQ. Here's the formula:

Your IQ = 100 + (Number of standard deviations below or above the average)*15

Now, let's define standard deviations by using an example. If we have 5 people with 5 different heights, then first we calculate the average. Let's say the average was 65 inches. The standard deviation is the "average distance" away from the average of each of the members. It is a direct measure of variability - if the 5 people included Jackie Chan and Shaquille O'Neal, obviously there's a lot more variability in that group than a group of 5 sisters who are all within 6 inches in height of each other. The standard deviation uses a number to characterize the average range of difference within a group.

A convenient feature of most groups is that they have a "normal" distribution- makes sense that most things would be normal, right? Without getting into a bunch of statistical mumbo-jumbo, you just need to know that if you know the average of the group and the standard deviation, you can successfully predict someone's percentile rank in the group.

Confused? Let me give you an example. If instead of 5 people's heights, we had 100 people, we could figure out their rank in height JUST by knowing the average, standard deviation, and their height. We wouldn't need to know each person's height and manually rank them, we could just predict their rank based on three numbers.

What this means is that you can take your PERCENTILE rank that is often given with your test and relate this to your RELATIVE IQ of people taking the test - that is, your IQ relative to the people taking the test. Obviously, there's no way to know your actual IQ because the people taking a standardized test are usually not very good samples of the general population- many of those with extremely low IQ's never achieve a level of success or competency necessary to complete a typical standardized test. In fact, professional psychologists who measure IQ actually have to use non-written tests that can fairly measure the IQ of those not able to complete a traditional test.

The bottom line is to not take your test score too seriously, but it is fun to compute your "relative IQ" among the people who took the test with you. I've done the calculations below. Just look up your percentile rank in the left and then you'll see your "relative IQ" for your test in the right hand column-

Percentile Rank	Your Relative IQ		Percentile Rank	Your Relative IQ
99	135		59	103
98	131		58	103
97	128		57	103
96	126		56	102
95	125		55	102
94	123		54	102
93	122		53	101
92	121		52	101
91	120		51	100
90	119		50	100
89	118		49	100
88	118		48	99
87	117		47	99
86	116		46	98
85	116		45	98
84	115		44	98
83	114		43	97
82	114		42	97
81	113		41	97
80	113		40	96
79	112		39	96
78	112		38	95
77	111		37	95
76	111		36	95
75	110		35	94
74	110		34	94
73	109		33	93
72	109		32	93
71	108		31	93
70	108		30	92
69	107		29	92
68	107		28	91
67	107		27	91
66	106		26	90
65	106		25	90
64	105		24	89
63	105		23	89
62	105		22	88
61	104		21	88
60	104		20	87

Special Report: What is Test Anxiety and How to Overcome It?

The very nature of tests caters to some level of anxiety, nervousness or tension, just as we feel for any important event that occurs in our lives. A little bit of anxiety or nervousness can be a good thing. It helps us with motivation, and makes achievement just that much sweeter. However, too much anxiety can be a problem; especially if it hinders our ability to function and perform.

"Test anxiety," is the term that refers to the emotional reactions that some test-takers experience when faced with a test or exam. Having a fear of testing and exams is based upon a rational fear, since the test-taker's performance can shape the course of an academic career. Nevertheless, experiencing excessive fear of examinations will only interfere with the test-takers ability to perform and his/her chances to be successful.

There are a large variety of causes that can contribute to the development and sensation of test anxiety. These include, but are not limited to lack of performance and worrying about issues surrounding the test.

Lack of Preparation

Lack of preparation can be identified by the following behaviors or situations:
- Not scheduling enough time to study, and therefore cramming the night before the test or exam
- Managing time poorly, to create the sensation that there is not enough time to do everything

Failing to organize the text information in advance, so that the study material consists of the entire text and not simply the pertinent information
Poor overall studying habits

Worrying, on the other hand, can be related to either the test taker, or many other factors around him/her that will be affected by the results of the test. These include worrying about:

Previous performances on similar exams, or exams in general
How friends and other students are achieving
The negative consequences that will result from a poor grade or failure

There are three primary elements to test anxiety. 1) Physical components, which involve the same typical bodily reactions as those to acute anxiety (to be discussed below). 2) Emotional factors have to do with fear or panic, and 3) Mental or cognitive issues concerning attention spans and memory abilities.

Physical Signals

There are many different symptoms of test anxiety, and these are not limited to mental and emotional strain. Frequently there are a range of physical signals that will let a test taker know that he/she is suffering from test anxiety. These bodily changes can include the following:

Perspiring
Sweaty palms
Wet, trembling hands
Nausea
Dry mouth
A knot in the stomach
Headache
Faintness
Muscle tension
Aching shoulders, back and neck
Rapid heart beat
Feeling too hot/cold

To recognize the sensation of test anxiety, a test-taker should monitor himself/herself for the following sensations:
- The physical distress symptoms as listed above
- Emotional sensitivity, expressing emotional feelings such as the need to cry or laugh too much, or a sensation of anger or helplessness
- A decreased ability to think, causing the test-taker to blank out or have racing thoughts that are hard to organize or control.

Though most students will feel some level of anxiety when faced with a test or exam, the majority can cope with that anxiety and maintain it at a manageable level. However, those who cannot are faced with a very real and very serious condition, which can and should be controlled for the immeasurable benefit of this sufferer.

Naturally, these sensations lead to negative results for the testing experience. The most common effects of test anxiety have to do with nervousness and mental blocking.

Nervousness

Nervousness can appear in several different levels:
- The test-taker's difficulty, or even inability to read and understand the questions on the test
- The difficulty or inability to organize thoughts to a coherent form
- The difficulty or inability to recall key words and concepts relating to the testing questions (especially essays)
- The receipt of poor grades on a test, though the test material was well known by the test taker

Conversely, a person may also experience mental blocking, which involves:

- Blanking out on test questions
- Only remembering the correct answers to the questions when the test has already finished.

Fortunately for test anxiety sufferers, beating these feelings, to a large degree, has to do with proper preparation. When a test taker has a feeling of preparedness, then anxiety will be dramatically lessened.

The first step to resolving anxiety issues is to distinguish which of the two types of anxiety are being suffered. If the anxiety is a direct result of a lack of preparation, this should be considered a normal reaction, and the anxiety level (as opposed to the test results) shouldn't be anything to worry about. However, if, when adequately prepared, the test-taker still panics, blanks out, or seems to overreact, this is not a fully rational reaction. While this can be considered normal too, there are many ways to combat and overcome these effects.

Remember that anxiety cannot be entirely eliminated; however, there are ways to minimize it, to make the anxiety easier to manage. Preparation is one of the best ways to minimize test anxiety. Therefore the following techniques are wise in order to best fight off any anxiety that may want to build.

To begin with, try to avoid cramming before a test, whenever it is possible. By trying to memorize an entire term's worth of information in one day, you'll be shocking your system, and not giving yourself a very good chance to absorb the information. This is an easy path to anxiety, so for those who suffer from test anxiety, cramming should not even be considered an option.

Instead of cramming, work throughout the semester to combine all of the material which is presented throughout the semester, and work on it gradually as the course goes by, making sure to master the main concepts first, leaving minor details for a week or so before the test.

To study for the upcoming exam, be sure to pose questions that may be on the examination, to gauge the ability to answer them by integrating the ideas from your texts, notes and lectures, as well as any supplementary readings.

If it is truly impossible to cover all of the information that was covered in that particular term, concentrate on the most important portions that can be covered very well. Learn these concepts as best as possible, so that when the test comes, a goal can be made to use these concepts as presentations of your knowledge.

In addition to study habits, changes in attitude are critical to beating a struggle with test anxiety. In fact, an improvement of the perspective over the entire test-taking experience can actually help a test taker to enjoy studying and therefore improve the overall experience. Be certain not to overemphasize the significance of the grade - know that the result of the test is neither a reflection of self worth, nor is it a measure of intelligence; one grade will not predict a person's future success.

To improve an overall testing outlook, the following steps should be tried:

- Keeping in mind that the most reasonable expectation for taking a test is to expect to try to demonstrate as much of what you know as you possibly can.
- Reminding ourselves that a test is only one test; this is not the only one, and there will be others.
- The thought of thinking of oneself in an irrational, all-or-nothing term should be avoided at all costs.

A reward should be designated for after the test, so there's something to look forward to. Whether it be going to a movie, going out to eat, or simply visiting friends, schedule it in advance, and do it no matter what result is expected on the exam.

Test-takers should also keep in mind that the basics are some of the most important things, even beyond anti-anxiety techniques and studying. Never neglect the basic social, emotional and biological needs, in order to try to absorb information. In order to best achieve, these three factors must be held as just as important as the studying itself.

Study Steps

Remember the following important steps for studying:
1. Maintain healthy nutrition and exercise habits. Continue both your recreational activities and social pass times. These both contribute to your physical and emotional well being.
2. Be certain to get a good amount of sleep, especially the night before the test, because when you're overtired you are not able to perform to the best of your best ability.
3. Keep the studying pace to a moderate level by taking breaks when they are needed, and varying the work whenever possible, to keep the mind fresh instead of getting bored.
4. When enough studying has been done that all the material that can be learned has been learned, and the test taker is prepared for the test, stop studying and do something relaxing such as listening to music, watching a movie, or taking a warm bubble bath.

There are also many other techniques to minimize the uneasiness or apprehension that is experienced along with test anxiety before, during, or even after the examination. In fact, there are a great deal of things that can be done to stop anxiety from interfering with lifestyle and performance. Again, remember that anxiety will not be eliminated entirely, and it shouldn't be. Otherwise that "up" feeling for exams would not exist, and most of us depend on that sensation to perform better than usual. However, this anxiety has to be at a level that is manageable.

Of course, as we have just discussed, being prepared for the exam is half the battle right away. Attending all classes, finding out what knowledge will be expected on the exam, and knowing the exam schedules are easy steps to lowering anxiety. Keeping up with work will remove the need to cram, and efficient study habits will eliminate wasted time. Studying should be done in an ideal location for concentration, so that it is simple to become interested in the material and give it complete attention. A method such as SQ3R (Survey, Question, Read, Recite, Review) is a wonderful key to follow to make sure that the study habits are as effective as possible, especially in the case of learning from a textbook.

Flashcards are great techniques for memorization. Learning to take good notes will mean that notes will be full of useful information, so that less sifting will need to be done to seek out what is pertinent for studying. Reviewing notes after class and then again on occasion will keep the information fresh in the mind. From notes that have been taken summary sheets and outlines can be made for simpler reviewing.

A study group can also be a very motivational and helpful place to study, as there will be a sharing of ideas, all of the minds can work together, to make sure that everyone understands, and the studying will be made more interesting because it will be a social occasion.

Basically, though, as long as the test-taker remains organized and self confident, with efficient study habits, less time will need to be spent studying, and higher grades will be achieved.

To become self-confident, there are many useful steps. The first of these is "self talk." It has been shown through extensive research, that self-talk for students who suffer from test anxiety, should be well monitored, in order to make sure that it contributes to self confidence as opposed to sinking the student. Frequently the self talk of test-anxious students is negative or self-defeating, thinking that everyone else is smarter and faster, that they always mess up, and that if they don't do well, they'll fail the entire course. It is important to decreasing anxiety that awareness is made of self talk. Try writing any negative self thoughts and then disputing them with a positive statement instead. Begin self-encouragement as though it was a friend speaking. Repeat positive statements to help reprogram the mind to believing in successes instead of failures.

Helpful Techniques

Other extremely helpful techniques include:

Self-visualization of doing well and reaching goals

While aiming for an "A" level of understanding, don't try to "overprotect" by setting your expectations lower. This will only convince the mind to stop studying in order to meet the lower expectations.

Don't make comparisons with the results or habits of other students. These are individual factors, and different things work for different people, causing different results.

Strive to become an expert in learning what works well, and what can be done in order to improve. Consider collecting this data in a journal.

Create rewards for after studying instead of doing things before studying that will only turn into avoidance behaviors.
Make a practice of relaxing - by using methods such as progressive relaxation, self-hypnosis, guided imagery, etc - in order to make relaxation an automatic sensation.

Work on creating a state of relaxed concentration so that concentrating will take on the focus of the mind, so that none will be wasted on worrying.

Take good care of the physical self by eating well and getting enough sleep.

Plan time in for exercise and stick to this plan.

Beyond these techniques, there are other methods to be used before, during and after the test that will help the test-taker perform well in addition to overcoming anxiety.

Before the exam comes the academic preparation. This involves establishing a study schedule and beginning at least one week before the actual date of the test. By doing this, the anxiety of not having enough time to study for the test will be automatically eliminated. Moreover, this will make the studying a much more effective experience, ensuring that the learning will be an easier process. This relieves much undue pressure on the test-taker.

Summary sheets, note cards, and flash cards with the main concepts and examples of these main concepts should be prepared in advance of the actual studying time. A topic should never be eliminated from this process. By omitting a topic because it isn't expected to be on the test is only setting up the test-taker for anxiety should it actually appear on the exam. Utilize the course syllabus for laying out the topics that should be studied. Carefully go over the notes that were made in class, paying special attention to any of the issues that the professor took special care to emphasize while lecturing in class. In the textbooks, use the chapter review, or if possible, the chapter tests, to begin your review.

It may even be possible to ask the instructor what information will be covered on the exam, or what the format of the exam will be (for example, multiple choice, essay, free form, true-false). Additionally, see if it is possible to find out how many questions will be on the test. If a review sheet or sample test has been offered by the professor, make good use of it, above anything else, for the preparation for the test. Another great resource for getting to know the examination is reviewing tests from previous semesters. Use these tests to review, and aim to achieve a 100% score on each of the possible topics. With a few exceptions, the goal that you set for yourself is the highest one that you will reach.

Take all of the questions that were assigned as homework, and rework them to any other possible course material. The more problems reworked, the more skill and confidence will form as a result. When forming the solution to a problem, write out each of the steps. Don't simply do head work. By doing as many steps on paper as possible, much clarification and therefore confidence will be formed. Do this with as many homework problems as possible, before checking the answers. By checking the answer after each problem, reinforcement will exist, that will not be on the exam. Study situations should be as exam-like as possible, to prime the test-taker's system for the experience. By waiting to check the answers at the end, a psychological advantage will be formed, to decrease the stress factor.

Another fantastic reason for not cramming is the avoidance of confusion in concepts, especially when it comes to mathematics. 8-10 hours of study will become one hundred percent more effective if it is spread out over a week or at least several days, instead of doing it all in one sitting. Recognize that the human brain requires time in order to assimilate new material, so frequent breaks and a span of study time over several days will be much more beneficial.

Additionally, don't study right up until the point of the exam. Studying should stop a minimum of one hour before the exam begins. This allows the brain to rest and put things in their proper order. This will also provide the time to become as relaxed as possible when going into the examination room. The test-taker will also have time to eat well and eat sensibly. Know that the brain needs food as much as the rest of the body. With enough food and enough sleep, as well as a relaxed attitude, the body and the mind are primed for success.

Avoid any anxious classmates who are talking about the exam. These students only spread anxiety, and are not worth sharing the anxious sentimentalities.

Before the test also involves creating a positive attitude, so mental preparation should also be a point of concentration. There are many keys to creating a positive attitude. Should fears become rushing in, make a visualization of taking the exam, doing well, and seeing an A written on the paper. Write out a list of affirmations that will bring a feeling of confidence, such as "I am doing well in my English class," "I studied well and know my material," "I enjoy this class." Even if the affirmations aren't believed at first, it sends a positive message to the subconscious which will result in an alteration of the overall belief system, which is the system that creates reality.

If a sensation of panic begins, work with the fear and imagine the very worst! Work through the entire scenario of not passing the test, failing the entire course, and dropping out of school, followed by not getting a job, and pushing a shopping cart through the dark alley where you'll live. This will place things into perspective! Then, practice deep breathing and create a visualization of the opposite situation - achieving an "A" on the exam, passing the entire course, receiving the degree at a graduation ceremony.

On the day of the test, there are many things to be done to ensure the best results, as well as the most calm outlook. The following stages are suggested in order to maximize test-taking potential:
- Begin the examination day with a moderate breakfast, and avoid any coffee or beverages with caffeine if the test taker is prone to jitters. Even people who are used to managing caffeine can feel jittery or light-headed when it is taken on a test day.
- Attempt to do something that is relaxing before the examination begins. As last minute cramming clouds the mastering of overall concepts, it is better to use this time to create a calming outlook.
- Be certain to arrive at the test location well in advance, in order to provide time to select a location that is away from doors, windows and other distractions, as well as giving enough time to relax before the test begins.
- Keep away from anxiety generating classmates who will upset the sensation of stability and relaxation that is being attempted before the exam.
- Should the waiting period before the exam begins cause anxiety; create a self-distraction by reading a light magazine or something else that is relaxing and simple.

During the exam itself, read the entire exam from beginning to end, and find out how much time should be allotted to each individual problem. Once writing the exam, should more time be taken for a problem, it should be abandoned, in order to begin another problem. If there is time at the end, the unfinished problem can always be returned to and completed.

Read the instructions very carefully - twice - so that unpleasant surprises won't follow during or after the exam has ended.

When writing the exam, pretend that the situation is actually simply the completion of homework within a library, or at home. This will assist in forming a relaxed atmosphere, and will allow the brain extra focus for the complex thinking function.

Begin the exam with all of the questions with which the most confidence is felt. This will build the confidence level regarding the entire exam and will begin a quality momentum. This will also create encouragement for trying the problems where uncertainty resides.

Going with the "gut instinct" is always the way to go when solving a problem. Second guessing should be avoided at all costs. Have confidence in the ability to do well. For essay questions, create an outline in advance that will keep the mind organized and make certain that all of the points are remembered. For multiple choice, read every answer, even if the correct one has been spotted - a better one may exist.

Continue at a pace that is reasonable and not rushed, in order to be able to work carefully. Provide enough time to go over the answers at the end, to check for small errors that can be corrected.

Should a feeling of panic begin, breathe deeply, and think of the feeling of the body releasing sand through its pores. Visualize a calm, peaceful place, and include all of the sights, sounds and sensations of this image. Continue the deep breathing, and take a few minutes to continue this with closed eyes. When all is well again, return to the test.

If a "blanking" occurs for a certain question, skip it and move on to the next question. There will be time to return to the other question later. Get everything done that can be done, first, to guarantee all the grades that can be compiled, and to build all of the confidence possible. Then return to the weaker questions to build the marks from there.

Remember, one's own reality can be created, so as long as the belief is there, success will follow. And remember: anxiety can happen later, right now, there's an exam to be written!

After the examination is complete, whether there is a feeling for a good grade or a bad grade, don't dwell on the exam, and be certain to follow through on the reward that was promised…and enjoy it! Don't dwell on any mistakes that have been made, as there is nothing that can be done at this point anyway.

Additionally, don't begin to study for the next test right away. Do something relaxing for a while, and let the mind relax and prepare itself to begin absorbing information again.

From the results of the exam - both the grade and the entire experience, be certain to learn from what has gone on. Perfect studying habits and work some more on confidence in order to make the next examination experience even better than the last one.

Learn to avoid places where openings occurred for laziness, procrastination and day dreaming.

Use the time between this exam and the next one to learn to relax better (even learning to relax on cue), so that any anxiety can be controlled during the next exam. Learn how to relax the body. Slouch in your chair if that helps. Tighten and then relax all of the different muscle groups, one group at a time, beginning with the feet and then working all the way up to the neck and face. This will ultimately relax the muscles more than they were to begin with. Learn how to breathe deeply and comfortably, and focus on this breathing going in and out as a relaxing thought. With every exhale, repeat the word "relax."

As common as test anxiety is, it is very possible to overcome it. Make yourself one of the test-takers who overcome this frustrating hindrance.

Special Report: Retaking the Test: What Are Your Chances at Improving Your Score?

After going through the experience of taking a major test, many test takers feel that once is enough. The test usually comes during a period of transition in the test taker's life, and taking the test is only one of a series of important events. With so many distractions and conflicting recommendations, it may be difficult for a test taker to rationally determine whether or not he should retake the test after viewing his scores.

The importance of the test usually only adds to the burden of the retake decision. However, don't be swayed by emotion. There a few simple questions that you can ask yourself to guide you as you try to determine whether a retake would improve your score:

1. What went wrong? Why wasn't your score what you expected?

Can you point to a single factor or problem that you feel caused the low score? Were you sick on test day? Was there an emotional upheaval in your life that caused a distraction? Were you late for the test or not able to use the full time allotment? If you can point to any of these specific, individual problems, then a retake should definitely be considered.

2. Is there enough time to improve?

Many problems that may show up in your score report may take a lot of time for improvement. A deficiency in a particular math skill may require weeks or months of tutoring and studying to improve. If you have enough time to improve an identified weakness, then a retake should definitely be considered.

3. How will additional scores be used? Will a score average, highest score, or most recent score be used?

Different test scores may be handled completely differently. If you've taken the test multiple times, sometimes your highest score is used, sometimes your average score is computed and used, and sometimes your most recent score is used. Make sure you understand what method will be used to evaluate your scores, and use that to help you determine whether a retake should be considered.

4. Are my practice tests scores significantly higher than my actual test score?

If you have taken a lot of practice tests and are consistently scoring at a much higher level than your actual test score, then you should consider a retake. However, if you've taken five practice tests and only one of your scores was higher than your actual test score, or if your practice tests scores was only slightly higher than your actual test score, then it is unlikely that you will significantly increase your score.

5. Do I need perfect scores or will I be able to live with this score? Will this score still allow me to follow my dreams?

What kind of score is acceptable to you? Is your current score "good enough?" Do you have to have a certain score in order to pursue the future of your dreams? If you won't be happy with your current score, and there's no way that you could live with it, then you should consider a retake. However, don't get your hopes up. If you are looking for significant improvement, that may or may not be possible. But if you won't be happy otherwise, it is at least worth the effort.

Remember that there are other considerations. To achieve your dream, it is likely that your grades may also be taken into account. A great test score is usually not the only thing necessary to succeed. Make sure that you aren't overemphasizing the importance of a high test score.

Furthermore, a retake does not always result in a higher score. Some test takers will score lower on a retake, rather than higher. One study shows that one-fourth of test takers will achieve a significant improvement in test score, while one-sixth of test takers will actually show a decrease. While this shows that most test takers will improve, the majority will only improve their scores a little and a retake may not be worth the test taker's effort.

Finally, if a test is taken only once and is considered in the added context of good grades on the part of a test taker, the person reviewing the grades and scores may be tempted to assume that the test taker just had a bad day while taking the test, and may discount the low test score in favor of the high grades. But if the test is retaken and the scores are approximately the same, then the validity of the low scores are only confirmed. Therefore, a retake could actually hurt a test taker by definitely bracketing a test taker's score ability to a limited range.

Special Report: Additional Bonus Material

Due to our efforts to try to keep this book to a manageable length, we've created a link that will give you access to all of your additional bonus material.

Please visit http://www.mometrix.com/bonus948/texestheatre to access the information.